# Friendship Leadership

# Friendship Leadership

**Matt Messner**

*and*

**Rachel McMurray-Branscombe**

*John & Nancy —*
*God - bless !*

WIPF & STOCK · Eugene, Oregon

Friendship Leadership

Wipf & Stock
An Imprint of Wipf and Stock Publishers
199 W. 8th Ave., Suite 3
Eugene, OR 97401

www.wipfandstock.com

PAPERBACK ISBN: 978-1-5326-6594-3
HARDCOVER ISBN: 978-1-5326-6595-0
EBOOK ISBN: 978-1-5326-6596-7

Manufactured in the U.S.A.                    10/24/18

# Contents

*Introduction* | vii

**PART 1: DISCOVERING FRIENDSHIP LEADERSHIP**

1. The Story of a Friend | 3

2. The Christian Legacy of Friendship Leadership | 9

**PART 2: PRACTICING FRIENDSHIP LEADERSHIP**

3. Friendship Leadership Defined | 31

4. The Benefits of Friendship Leadership | 39

5. Qualities in Friendship Leadership | 50

6. People in Friendship Leadership | 78

**PART 3: EMPOWERING FRIENDSHIP LEADERSHIP**

7. When Friendship Hurts | 95

8. Dual Relationships | 108

9. Friendship Leadership in High Power Distance Cultures | 111

10. Cross-Attraction Friendship Leadership | 123

11. The Introverted Leader Friend | 135

12. Conclusion | 147

*Discussion Questions* | 151
*Bibliography* | 157

# Introduction

THE QUALITY OF ONE's life is directly proportionate to the quality of one's friendships. As an organizational leader I have felt and observed a shift from an emphasis on results to an emphasis on relationships. Leaders are focusing more on people, instead of power. We want to live lives that are more value-driven than purpose-or profit-driven. These leaders are interested in experiencing work environments that are professional, productive and personal. Too often "leadership" exerts itself through hierarchical power and control. A revolution of friendship is reshaping organizations from within, and when we resist this reality, we resist a future of opportunities. Instead, we should strive to understand, embrace and implement this new philosophy of leadership in order to form a more dynamic, attractive and impactful culture.

After three days of voracious note-taking, I felt as if I was ready to change the world. Or at least our community. As I stood on the moving walkway, making my way through the airport, I reflected on the conference—the speakers had inspired me with their deluge of success stories. They had given me clear and simple strategies for multiplying my influence. The conference had featured non-stop inspiring entertainment that had awakened my creativity while keeping me fully engaged. The expense of the trip was going to be worth it—I had been transformed as a leader.

But three days later, after transposing a few notes into my calendar, I placed the conference notebook onto my bookshelf where it sat alongside a dozen similar leadership-themed notebooks (filled with notes that I had taken in the past at other "life-changing" conferences or seminars), all untouched, covered with a fine layer of dust.

In that moment, I felt duped. It had been a good conference, but it might not have changed me. Furthermore, it might not have made me a better leader.

I looked in the proverbial mirror and asked myself the cold hard question that every leader must be able to answer, *"Where does lasting influence really come from?"* I faced this fact: it wasn't coming from my shelf of notebooks.

This crucial question brought things suddenly into focus. The answer was simple, obvious and clear: *People had been the primary influencers on my life.* I immediately thought of three people who had one thing in common.

## Andy

It was the "totally awesome" year of 1985. The music was over-synthesized, the fashion was terrible, and I was 16 years old. My parents had just moved our family to beautiful Bend, Oregon, a town nestled in the middle of the state at the foot of the Cascade Mountains. Like other 16-year-olds, I was trying to find myself with a fierce determination that I can only liken to dangerously stumbling around in the dark. I hoped that by achieving "success," I would find acceptance and happiness. All I had to do was arrive at that place of success.

Distance running may be a fringe sport, but that did not deter me from pursuing it with abandonment. The pursuit of happiness is a right the founders of the United States died to give us, but as I chased that elusive dream I came up empty-handed. No level of success satisfied my soul. It was an important lesson to learn at the age of 16. Winning a state championship in cross-country did not deliver the happiness that I had anticipated.

If success wasn't going to bring the happiness that I was looking for, I decided to look elsewhere. My classmates seemed to enjoy the party scene, so I delved into that, abandoning my values in case they had been keeping me from what I really needed. Of course, this only led me into a further sense of misery.

I was spiritually empty. Actually depressed. I was being crushed by the pressure of my own impossible expectations.

While this was going on I became friends with a classmate and neighbor named Andy. He had his own car and I preferred getting a ride to school over catching the bus.

Riding to school with him began to influence me. He introduced me to a new band called U2 and I started tagging along as he attended meetings of a Christian club called Young Life. This awakened within me a deep spiritual hunger that placed me on a path towards God. I started going to church with him, as well. While on this common path, we both had a profound and life-altering awakening of faith. We discussed the Bible. We prayed for our classmates. We shared our struggles and our failures with each other.

Two years later we ended up attending the same small Bible college in Southern California where we were college roommates. Our future wives were also roommates and today Andy and I are both pastors in the same denomination. He had a lasting influence on my life.

## Dave

Dave was a missionary who was back home in Los Angeles and lived a block away from the Bible college I was attending. He had been living in Nigeria and now made his base in L.A. He came by the dorm one day looking for people to join him in running. So it began. Then Dave urged me to run the L.A. Marathon. I tried to explain to him that I was a runner but not a marathon runner (and there is a big difference). He was undeterred. I agreed to begin training with him a couple of times a week and we began logging miles together on the trails around Dodger stadium as I prepared for my first marathon (a decision that changed my life).

During one of our runs I remember Dave talking to me about how God works through relationships more than anything else. As a young Christian, it was a new paradigm for me, challenging my introverted tendency and shifting my gaze from my books towards people. Since then I have never stopped looking at how God is always using people—establishing friendships and strategically bringing us together—in order to accomplish His greater purposes in my life and the lives of others.

Because of Dave, I would go on to run a total of 18 marathons. We would cover countless miles together, wherever and whenever our paths would cross. More significantly, he became a lifelong friend. The conversations and the prayers that took place on the trails and the streets that we ran were life-changing and life-shaping.

## Jerry

Jerry was the closest thing to Jesus that I had ever met with skin on. He had pastored a great church. He had written books. He was a wonderful teacher and a brilliant speaker. Everyone wanted to be mentored by Jerry. He was much older than me; semi-retired and a very active grandpa. I had learned a lot from him through his books and classes.

But his greatest influence in my life did not take place in a classroom or a pew. I felt it quietly, while standing waist deep in icy streams, casting flies to suspicious trout. It happened while riding the ferry to islands that contained secrets that only Jerry knew about. His influence grew over breakfast in backwoods diners at the crack of dawn when the fish were just starting to wake up. His leadership in my life was found in the activities of building a fly rod, paddling pontoon boats around still lakes, cooking around a campfire and driving to fishing holes—this is where I felt that his wisdom had its full impact on my life.

We became friends, and as we did, our friendship changed me.

The common factor in all three of these relationships: friendship.

These experiences and reflections guided me towards a deeper study of the relationship between friendship and leadership. I started having intentional conversations on this subject and seeing things in the Bible that I had overlooked. Eventually, I was compelled to make this the subject of my doctoral studies. The deeper I dug, the more convinced I became, that friendship is an essential and powerful ingredient in transformational leadership.

# PART 1

Discovering Friendship Leadership

# 1

## The Story of a Friend

IN THE BEGINNING, GOD walked with Adam and Eve. As they strolled in the cool of the day, they wandered among fruit trees and along unexplored paths—the oasis in the desert. They spoke of creation and the garden in its splendor. Together, they experienced the wonder thriving in the details of a flower petal, the vastness of existence, the sound of moving water, and the stillness of an afternoon passed in each other's company. They made this choice: to spend time together, to build a deep and intimate relationship, unique to them.

In the beginning, there was friendship, and with it, the possibility of pain. With that choice of friendship, there was also an implicit choice to remain vulnerable, open to love and hurt. One day, this friendship was marred by betrayal, the choice of power over relationship. Heaven roared with the grief of it, for this was not mere disobedience, but the rupture of sacred friendship.

But then, in what could be described as the miracle enlaced within each friendship, forgiveness made a way for reconciliation, for hope. Impossible as it may seem, God who walked with Adam and Eve in the garden chose to continue walking with them, even after they left the sacred boundaries of heaven-on-earth. These, our ancestors, felt the living presence of the creator through his enduring presence in their life. He was, after all, their Friend.

Though everything in creation had a relationship with the creator, God continued to extend himself toward humankind, in the openness of free will and choice. Would they choose to love him back, choose vulnerability and dependence, even as he held their very world together?

Some embraced this friendship, and were so-called friends of God.

There was a man, Abraham, humble in nature, imperfect but honest. His immediate family was a small one—just he and his wife, Sarah, (though he had quite a few extended relatives). God made himself known to Abraham, first through a command, then through a promise. First, as Lord, then as Friend. The all-powerful, the all-knowing, entered into a commitment with a human: unnecessary for obedience; necessary for intimacy. Mutual trust flowered between Abraham and God through decades of walking together, wakeful dreams, and fulfilled words.

He wanted to encourage these friends as he led them, so God spoke through human form, visiting both Abraham and Sarah. How many times did their Friend remind them of the promise, the hope of future generations? How sensitive a Friend to care about their feelings, even as they waited. As their leader, God wasn't content to issue a command, then abandon his friends to the long-suffering process of waiting—he joined them in the process, offering all he could (his counsel, encouragement, presence), as they practiced patience.

This same Friend consulted with Abraham when considering the fate of Sodom, allowing the man with whom God had shared a decades-long intimacy with to influence future actions. From destruction (*"Far be it from you to do such a thing!"* Gen 18:25) to redemption for those faithful, Abraham spoke to the Friend who had been walking alongside him for years, the Friend he knew to be merciful and just, right and good. And though he was God, the Creator listened to his friend and mercy dwelt within that moment.

Years and generations later, a young heart sought out an old Friend. On rocky hilltops, in shadowed valleys, over miles of yellow dirt speckled with faint traces of green vegetation, a lonely young shepherd (famous to us now, but overlooked then), discovered intimacy in warm, quiet companionship. A voice, clear and pure, called out from the emptiness of isolation into the unknown universe, wanting to *be known*. This call for companionship found its response in the Almighty God. David, the young shepherd, encountered the kind of friendship that looked deeper than the surface, saw what was and what could—*would*—be. When God became David's friend, He called out the truth of the individual and named the inner identity of David. God befriended a rough, uneducated youth before he had anything to offer, before he was a "somebody." And David chose God as his friend, investing hours in the pursuit of the One he felt surrounding him. He was *known*, there in the pasturelands, and he also began the process of knowing

God—his true friend. Instead of barren valleys and silent hills, the world was filled with the mystery of friendship.

Called out of the desert and into the palace, David then discovered the miracle at the heart of all true selfless friendships: what we receive becomes that which we can offer to others. Friendship is a multiplying force. What began as a friendship between God and a lowly shepherd was then reflected in the friendship between a court musician and a prince. Loyalty and commitment colored the relationship of David and Jonathan. Intimacy and respect gave it life. As David knew God and was known by him, he also knew Jonathan and Jonathan knew him. It was a friendship of one spirit, one love. Their friendship was a covenant to build up, to protect—a covenant that characterizes the deepest, most God-like love.

But there was another in the young shepherd's life, one who did *not* experience friendship with the great Friend. No matter how much power he hoarded, how much fear he instilled, Saul could never find the peace in relationship. He was friendless, for what he did not allow himself to experience with God, he could not offer as an experience to others under his leadership. Did he have the title? Certainly. The authority? Absolutely. Good looks? Riches? Armies? All, yes. But without friendship, Saul's leadership faltered. Yet somewhere, miles away from Saul's stately home, hiding in a damp cave, David's leadership continued to strengthen, as mighty men grew to know their leader as their friend.

Like all experienced relationships, the friendship between David and his Creator-Friend was tested through time and temptation, through grief and grace. The friendship that has not withstood the heart-tormenting reality of human fallacy and failure is but a mere shadow of the love and friendship God offers us. Each time David fell short of his commitment to friendship, both his friendship to God and those whom he led, he encountered the remarkable mercy only discovered in love. Though he had the authority and power of leadership for the rest of his life, we see in David a man who treasured his friendships with family, advisers, followers—making friends of them all. And this marked David as a truly notable leader, a man after God's own heart.

Over the centuries, through continued and deliberate relationships, one infused with vulnerability (for how many times was this Creator-Friend hurt?), God continued to lead his people. He spoke not as a tyrant, but as one who walks alongside. Those faithful few, who took up the call of friendship, being led through friendship, they walked with God.

And yet . . .

This Friend wanted to walk *alongside* us—not only in spirit, but in the flesh. So he took on our flesh, our skin and bones, our mortality. In the form of Jesus, God inhabited humanity.

∽

In all the world, he possessed only one thing: relationships.

He had grown up in a relatively small town, the kind where everyone knows everyone else. His father was a woodworker, and Jesus was raised to follow in the family business. Working with his hands, he knew of splinters and late hours, paying the family bills and satisfying customers. The community in which he grew up watched as he turned from a boy into a man, as all little boys must do.

But in his heart, he knew a change was coming. Unlike the other boys and girls who grew into men and women around him, the ones who married, settled down, and found life in a myriad of creature comforts, Jesus would have to leave it all behind, giving up the family business, the safety of a home community, the security of financial income, the promise of a quiet life and an assured future. He gave all this up and more, bringing only one thing with him on that long and dusty road: his friends.

When he set out in leadership, he was alone, a single figure approaching a river baptism. He was recognized, but all leaders know recognition isn't the same thing as being *known*. He endured temptation and rejection, performed miracles and healings—these qualifications alone would mark him as a once-in-a-generation prophet, leader, and minister. But he was more than all this: he was the Creator-Friend in person, looking for friends to join him on his journey (both literally and figuratively), over dusty roads and into dusty hearts. Then one day, by the sea, he found friends.

Their friendships began the way most do: slowly. To be known, truly *known*, takes time. He was leader *and* Friend. Known and being made known.

There were the twelve best friends, those who ate with him, slept on his right and left on cold nights outdoors, who heard the secrets of the universe even as they shared the most basic functions of life, like restroom breaks, joking, hunger-induced stomach rumblings, and foot blisters. These friendships were inspired by prayer and strengthened by covenant, formed through shared experience and necessary course-correction.

On one such occasion, the friends thought they knew the priorities of the Friend. (Doesn't this always happen in life? Well-meaning friends assuming wrong things?) Parents brought Jesus their small children for blessing and healing. The twelve best friends, thinking they were being helpful, turned them away. You see, their Friend's time was limited, too precious to waste on children who couldn't begin to understand the complexities of the teachings (or so went the logic of the friends). But the path of friendship, of knowing and being known, doesn't always travel in the direction we believe it does. We surprise and are surprised. But even in error, Jesus didn't lash out in anger, hurt by their good-intentioned but faulty assumptions. Neither was he insecure in their understanding or the future of their relationship. Their Leader-Friend addressed the error quickly, communicating gently and clearly.

Beyond these best friends pulsed a circle of friends who branched out into all walks of life. From the blue-collar fishermen to the elite Pharisees and tax collectors, men and women, Jesus built friendships on the foundation of his own initiative. He wept alongside mourners and ate countless meals with the desperate and lonely.

On one occasion, there were two sisters living as roommates who decided to make a new Friend. As is often the case with sisters, their personalities were opposite from one another. One sister, Martha, suffered under the societal pressure often lurking beneath ideas of friendship: a perfect show of hospitality (no dishes in the sink, expertly-prepared meal, dust-free windowsills, etc.). The other sister, Mary, simply sat and listened to her new Friend, knowing and being known. The Friend, compassion coloring observation, reminded Martha that friendship was not about presentation and performance but presence. He led Martha through that moment in the gentleness of friendship. All Jesus required of that moment was sharing life, knowing and being known.

Over the course of his leadership, he took every opportunity to honor relationship over rule-keeping: healing on the Sabbath, accepting the gift of anointing oil, encouraging the faith of those who had not deserved it. Unlike the other religious leaders who kept a more socially-acceptable wall between those with authority and those without it, Jesus assured his friends that all he had received, he had made known to them. While some leaders practiced intimacy deprivation, Jesus embodied intimacy overflow.

The rewards of such choices, however, were not without a deep cost. Would the Creator-Friend ever walk away from friendship unscathed?

Would such a friendship ever avoid the pains of betrayal? It doesn't appear so. From a lost garden at the beginning to a fire-lit courtyard at the end (if you listen, you can hear a rooster in the distance), the offer of friendship has always been met with the failings of humankind. We are not always deserving of friends, but friendship is offered nevertheless. We grasp hold of our Leader-Friend with teary eyes, finally realizing the cost of love.

For the Friend who had given up all earthly possessions, carrying only relationships along the journey, the ultimate betrayal and abandonment of almost all his friends was the last sacrifice he made, just before losing his life. Only one best friend showed at the cross. There were other friends at the end, however, and their names were not far from his lips as he uttered his last words. And then the world's first and only perfect Friend died.

If this was the end, we would be left wondering what all this says about Friendship Leadership. Was it worth it—when it only led to pain? It was bad enough Jesus had to sacrifice his life, but did he really have to undergo the heart-wrenching makes-you-sick-to-your-stomach betrayal and rejection of those whom he loved most? We would still be arguing these points today . . . if this was the end of the story.

But Jesus rose. He defeated death. At the turning point of all universal understanding, at the commencement of a new age of existence, where does he go first?

Back to his friends.

The same ones who betrayed him, who abandoned him, who doubted him. The friends who never really knew him, never really appreciated him. Those friends.

His first act as a resurrected God was to heal damaged friendships. To Mary, he gave joy. To Peter, forgiveness. To Thomas, reassurance. To everyone, peace and another chance at friendship.

Throughout the story, the Creator leads his people through friendship: from Adam to Peter, Abraham to Martha. Each was loved, invited into the intimate process of knowing and being known. Even as God desired a fuller expression of friendship in the person of Jesus, Jesus promised yet another form of the Leader-Friend: a spirit of truth who will walk alongside us forever. We are led by our Friend, and what we receive becomes that which we can offer to others. Friendship leadership is a multiplying force.

# 2

## The Christian Legacy of Friendship Leadership

"The little knots of *friends* who turn their backs on the 'World' are those who really transform it."[1]

C.S. LEWIS (EMPHASIS ADDED)

FRIENDS WORKING TOGETHER ARE the most effective influencers in the world. They have the power to exercise greater impact over individuals than family, bosses, and political powers. Their influence is very personal, current, active, and takes place within the immediate context of life. Their care, touch, and encouragement, all come together to form a powerful influence that shapes decisions and behavior as well as a person's psychological and spiritual perspective. Consequently, friends affect behavior within businesses, churches, families, and all other networks of people. Within the fabric of society, friendships form informal networks of power and potential that are often overlooked. These networks are the starting point for the creation of businesses, charities, clubs, schools, churches, and just about every organization that exists. People today are looking for caring and approachable leaders. They are looking for those with whom they will have a sense of walking on a mutually shared path. This is a subject of particular relevance for Christian leaders. Although this may seem obvious, some leaders still hesitate to offer what their followers crave. Pastors have become isolated from friendship, and have often been taught to keep "safely distant" from the people they lead and serve. Because of this, pastoral leaders are often left alone, lonely, and out of touch from the real

1. Lewis, *The Four Loves.*

needs of people. Not surprisingly, H.B. London Jr. has found that "most members of the clergy feel isolated, insecure, and only rarely affirmed."[2] "It's lonely at the top" is not merely a reality for pastors, as it is a common struggle for all leaders. Embracing Friendship Leadership, however, will break down these walls.

I have a few goals in this book:

- To challenge the idea that isolated leadership is acceptable for Christian leaders. Leadership effectiveness is closely tied to the inclusion of the ingredient of friendship. Part 1 demonstrates our biblical onus to Friendship Leadership.

- To develop a contrasting leadership style which emphasizes friendship. In Part 2, I offer a clear definition and description of this alternative form of leadership.

- To encourage Christian leaders on their path to make intentional friendship an important part of their leadership. In Part 3, we will look at both the barriers to Friendship Leadership, and the tools at our disposal.

Before we jump into the practical "whys" (believe me, there are several), we should begin by returning to the Bible and the story it provides us. It serves as the guide for our values, principles, and behaviors, and it should be the source from which we draw our primary inspiration. In this chapter, we'll look at a few passages of Scripture a little more closely to reexamine if "servant leadership" is the primary approach to leadership in Jesus' ministry, and then consider how Friendship Leadership continued on through the Christian tradition and history. Knowing the larger story to which we belong informs us of our role and the possibilities of relationship.

## On Closer Examination

Friendship is one of the major themes of the Bible. Within the canon are stories of friendships between people as well as examples of friendship between people and God. In fact, redemption itself made it possible for humankind to have a relationship with God that displays the characteristics of friendship, including encouragement, presence, fellowship, counsel, and much more.

2. Mills, "Who Ministers to the Minister?"

Redemption shows the extent to which God was willing to go in order to make it possible for humankind to be restored to a healthy relationship with God, from which healthy friendships can also be modeled and developed. Being created in the image of God, people long for relationship not only with God, but also with one another. It was God himself who stated, "It is not good for man to be alone." This assessment by God reflects the human need for companionship.

In the opening chapter, I focused on the relationship between God and us. It is the basis for all other relational realities. Without first recognizing God as the source of and method by which we live out love, we cannot hope to progress into the realm of human-to-human friendships. For this reason, the Bible gives us a narrative of this divine Friend, who walks alongside us. And building upon that, we also find examples within the text of how God-friendship inspired human friendship. It gives us stories and skills, poems and proverbs to utilize as we follow in the footsteps of our Friend.

Friendship is a God-given gift, and is an important part of every culture. This chapter will consider more fully a couple friendships in the Old and New Testaments, drawing specifics out of the Scripture for our consideration.

The Hebrew word for friend is *rea* (עְרֵמַ). This word appears 188 times in 173 verses of the Old Testament. Besides being translated "friend" in English, it is also translated as neighbor, companion, and fellow, depending on what English translation is being used. Its frequent usage demonstrates its prominence as a recurring theme. The Greek word translated as friend is *philos* (φίλος). When used as a verb, this word describes the action of loving. It is a word tied so closely to love that when translated "friend," there is the aspect of love and affection tied right into the word. In the Bible, it also describes an associate or companion.

## Snapshots of Friendship Leadership in the Old Testament

Friendship with God is a common Old Testament theme. The story of the creation of humankind speaks of God initiating relationship with those whom he made in his own image. Eve is created out of Adam to satisfy a pure desire for companionship. Other biblical characters' relationships with God are described in affectionate or intimate terms. Genesis 5:24 states that "Enoch walked with God; then he was no more, because God took him." Walking with God implies companionship and partnership. James 2:23

states that Abraham "was called God's friend." Moses' relationship with God was described in very intimate terms: "Since then, no prophet has risen in Israel like Moses, whom the Lord knew face to face," (Deut 34:10). This speaks of God's intimate knowledge of Moses and the great intimacy of their relationship. The Psalms are replete with intimate expressions of love and companionship between the Psalmist and God. These references and others combine to demonstrate the availability, reality, and desirability of friendship with God in the Old Testament.

## David and Jonathan

The Old Testament also describes some important friendships between people. One of most vivid examples of friendship in the Old Testament is the story of David and Jonathan. This narrative shows how rich, valuable, and precious friendship can be.

David and Jonathan were the deepest of friends—forging a bond that surpassed that of blood; they supported each other through the darkest of times. The powerful depth of this friendship is described well in First Samuel 18:1, "After David had finished talking with Saul, Jonathan became one in spirit with David, and he loved him as himself." This was his response to what he saw in David and heard from him as he talked to Saul about defeating Goliath. Jonathan's own exploits of faith in battle reflect a similar faith in action as that which was demonstrated by David. This affinity knit them together in the beginning of this friendship and kept them from any rivalry for power or position. David and Jonathan committed themselves to one another by making a covenant together on at least four occasions.[3] For David and Jonathan, their friendship was deepened through the establishment and renewal of their covenant with one another.

Jonathan said to David, "Go in peace, for we have sworn friendship with each other in the name of the Lord, saying, 'The Lord is witness between you and me, and between your descendants and my descendants forever.'"[4] At Jonathan's death, David cried out: "O Jonathan, in your death I am stricken, I am desolate for you, Jonathan my brother. Very dear to me you were, your love to me more wonderful than the love of a woman."[5] It was friendship that brought together David the shepherd and Jonathan the prince. Their kinship superseded the hierarchical expectations of the

3. First Sam 18:3, 20:17, 20:42, 23:18.

4. First Sam 20:42.

5. Second Sam 1:26.

monarchy as Jonathan pledged his support to David. Jonathan, motivated by friendship, worked to protect David, and it was their friendship that made David patient with Saul. This story provides us with a biblical example of the practical application of Friendship Leadership and the way God can use it supernaturally to accomplish his purposes.

We have more than a singular example from the life of David, however. Throughout the course of his leadership, we see a pattern of friendship. First Chronicles 11 records the powerful story of the three mighty men of David who risked their lives to bring David a drink of water from the well near the gate of Bethlehem. In the next chapter of First Chronicles, we're given the image of men who joined David's mission, full of the devotion and commitment that is forged in friendship, faith, and shared food. I think we all know that food isn't merely fuel for the body; it's fuel for friendship.

## The Wisdom Books

Is it any wonder, then, that the Psalms would reflect this deep value of friendship? The Psalms reveal the way a relationship with God can be one of deep personal communion. The terms of affection and endearment used in the praises of Israel are often so personal, emotional, and specific, that one would think the Psalmist was writing to a friend.

The book of Proverbs is so full of advice regarding friendship, that it could be called a "treatise on friendship."[6] Proverbs 18:24 reads, "A man of many companions may come to ruin, but there is a friend who sticks closer than a brother." This Proverb praises the value of friends, set in contrast to acquaintances. It also describes how friends can be more committed to each other than even family members. Friends often are stronger relationships than those of a family. Proverbs 17:17 reinforces this point further by stating, "A friend loves at all times, and a brother is born for adversity." The power of friendship is accentuated in a culture where families are broken and dysfunctional.

Proverbs stresses the importance of character and integrity in keeping friendships strong. Proverbs 16:28–29 warns, "A perverse man stirs up dissension, and a gossip separates close friends." This is a reminder of the importance of trust within a healthy friendship. Generosity is a quality that is useful in gaining friends. Proverbs 19:6–7 states, "Many curry favor with a ruler, and everyone is the friend of a man who gives gifts. A poor man

6. Black, *The Art of Being a Good Friend*, 21.

is shunned by all his relatives—how much more do his friends avoid him! Though he pursues them with pleading, they are nowhere to be found." Several other Proverbs address the use of money and generosity to gain and keep friends.

Friends are able to correct one another. Proverbs 27:5–6 makes this clear: "Better is open rebuke than hidden love. Wounds from a friend can be trusted, but an enemy multiplies kisses." Friends are often the only ones who have earned the right to correct and challenge people in a way that will be heard, taken seriously, and result in change. Reinforcing the value of the counsel of friends is Proverbs 27:9–10: "Perfume and incense bring joy to the heart, and the pleasantness of one's friend springs from his earnest counsel. Do not forsake your friend and the friend of your father." Friends are able to spur one another on towards greatness. Proverbs 27:17 states, "As iron sharpens iron, so one man sharpens another."

Many of these Proverbs warn against the pitfalls of false or unhealthy friendships that have the power to lead a person astray. These verses clearly present friendship as something to be prudently valued, kept, and cared for. The book of Proverbs shows that friendship "is possibly such a blessed relationship, a state of love and trust and generous comradeship, where a person feels safe to be himself, because he knows that he will not easily be misunderstood."[7] The following four points summarize a biblical view of friendship based on the book of Proverbs:

1. A righteous person is careful about who they choose as friends.

2. Friendship can be strengthened and broadened through generosity.

3. Friendship can be a stronger relationship than familial relationships.

4. Integrity of speech and honesty will help keep friendship strong.

One of the most popular passages in the book of Ecclesiastes is 4:9–12:

> Two are better than one, because they have a good return for their work: if one falls down, his friend can help him up. But pity the man who falls and has no one to help him up! Also, if two lie down together, they will keep warm. But how can one keep warm alone? Though one may be overpowered, two can defend themselves. A cord of three strands is not quickly broken.

This passage describes how a friend can aid in productivity, assistance, safety, provision, protection, and power. It reminds the reader of the

7. Black, *The Art of Being a Good Friend*, 21.

importance and the value of friendship, in very practical ways. From these Old Testament examples, the value of friendship can be clearly understood. It has been shown as a means for satisfying the innate human need for companionship, an expression of love in leadership.

## Snapshots of Friendship Leadership in the New Testament

In the previous chapter, we had the chance to appreciate the narrative of Jesus' friendships. I would like to examine further the characteristics that colored his friendships, as he utilized them throughout his ministry. The key verse of this ministry philosophy is the most powerful statement that Jesus ever made about friendship. It is found in John 15:13–16:

> "Greater love has no one than this, that he lay down his life for his friends. You are my friends if you do what I command. *I no longer call you servants, because a servant does not know his master's business. Instead, I have called you friends, for everything that I learned from my Father I have made known to you.* You did not choose me, but I chose you and appointed you to go and bear fruit— fruit that will last. Then the Father will give you whatever you ask in my name." (Emphasis added.)

In this statement, Jesus crowns friendship as the culmination of three years spent with his closest followers. Friendship was the outcome of his investment in their lives.

Though there can be multiple definitions of the Greek word used for friendship, it is in this passage that Jesus' definition becomes clear. For him, friendship was the progressive outcome of his relationship with the disciples. It developed through disclosure, which caused the relationship to progress from one of servitude to one of friendship. The disciples became friends because all that Jesus had heard from the Father he had made known to them. A "Lord" or "Master" will disclose only as much information as needed to get things done. But Jesus treated the disciples as friends by making "all things" known to them. This passage shows that Jesus characterized friendship as a relationship with a high level of trust and intimacy.

A close examination of the relationship between Jesus and his disciples is an interesting study on friendship. Jesus often referred to the disciples as his friends. They spent their time traveling together, walking together, eating together, praying together, and ministering together. In this relationship it seems as though Jesus was always the one taking the initiative. He invites them to follow him, and then invites them into a deep relationship. It was going to be a relationship of high priority for him, superseding even the natural bonds of family. Aspects of their relationship that gave it depth are:

1. Jesus spent time with them. They ate together, traveled together, prayed together, and ministered together.

2. Jesus shared the most painful moments of his experience with them. ("Then he said to them, 'My soul is overwhelmed with sorrow to the point of death. Stay here and keep watch with me," Matt 26:38.)

3. Jesus shared insights that were not disclosed to those outside their close circle of friendship (John 13:1–17).

4. Jesus humbled himself in offering acts of tender care and servitude.

5. Jesus offered the disciples emotional support when they faced fears and uncertainty. He was genuine in his concern for their feelings.

6. Together they experienced times of popularity and times of rejection.

7. Their relationship included confrontation, tension, misunderstanding, jealousy, disappointment, joy, betrayal, and forgiveness.

The account of the relationship between Jesus and his disciples reveals the firsthand knowledge that Jesus had about the positive and the negative aspects of becoming close to people. Jesus, as the model leader, did not seem concerned about dual relationships, keeping a distance from his disciples, or keeping the upper hand on them. Instead, he seemed to grow closer to them, and more invested in them, as time went on. Close friendships require an investment of time as well as shared experiences.

Jesus modeled a love that was inclusive, but at the same time he invested his time with wisdom. Scripture makes it clear that Jesus was very likable and charismatic, having friends beyond the twelve disciples, including Mary, Martha and Lazarus, publicans and sinners, and numerous others he encountered during his ministry. Jesus was an approachable leader. He drew people to himself: "In Jesus men saw friendship raised to its highest power, and the truth burst upon them —'This Friend must be God.'"[8]

In addition to the broad circle of friends and narrower circle of disciples, there were *the three*: James, John and Peter. And within even those three, there was "the disciple whom Jesus loved" (John 21:20). Regarding

8. Weatherhead, *The Transforming Friendship*, 125.

the disciple whom Jesus loved, John, it is an interesting fact to note that it was only John who identified himself by this term. Is it possible that the other disciples also felt like they were "the disciple whom Jesus loved"? It is certain that Jesus had a remarkable ability to be a friend, and he assigned friendship a high priority in his ministry. Jesus was able to love all people, unconditionally, having many friends, and extending love and compassion even to those he encountered for the first time. The ability to communicate and express love towards large numbers of people represents one level of being a friend. It is this kind of friendship that enhances the likeability, influence, and the compassion of a leader. It is an attribute to be sought after by every follower of Christ.

Still, even Jesus knew that a deeper investment could only be made in a select group of people. Jesus did this with twelve choice men, despite knowing their imperfections and failures, and even knowing one would betray him, another would deny him, and all would abandon him. The ability to only sustain a small number of close friendships is verified by modern research which has shown that on average, "a typical personal friendship network consists of 1–2 best friends, 4–6 close friends, and 10–20 casual friends."[9] The "circles" of friends that surrounded Jesus confirm the reality that some friendships will always be deeper than others. These are constraining aspects presented by the limits of time and culture. It is for this reason that being intentional is helpful in the formation and selection of friendships that can be invested in and nurtured. These decisions are for individuals to make carefully, prayerfully, and purposefully.

Leaders must accept their limitations in that they cannot be friends with everyone they are leading. This book is not meant to imply that a person can effectively befriend everyone in a large group over which they are exercising leadership. A leader may be able to take the disposition of a friend towards many people, or apply the qualities of friendship in a variety of situations, and by doing so, strengthen their ability to lead, but in doing so, some of the key components of friendship may be lacking. As was the case with Christ, strategic friendships must be identified, nurtured, and managed. These inner-circles of friendship will be the ones where the greatest degree of influence will take place.

Jesus challenged his followers to place a high priority on friendship. It was such a high priority that he called it a commandment. In John 13:34–35 he states, "I give you a new commandment, that you love one another. Just

9. Yager, *Who's That Sitting At My Desk?*, 48.

as I have loved you, you also should love one another. By this everyone will know that you are my disciples, if you have love for one another." This makes friendship an unavoidable prerogative in the life of every Christian. Leaders are called to live lives that model this behavior.

Similarly, "Love your neighbor as yourself," and "Do to others as you would have them do to you," are key commands that compel followers of Christ to place a high priority on the application of character qualities conducive to friendship: generosity, care, encouragement, service, empathy, loyalty, and respect. The relationships between followers of Christ are to be relationships characterized by love. It is a love intended to be unique, distinct, visible, and attractive. Having these kinds of relationships not only changes the recipients of the friendship, but it also has the potential to draw others to Christ by presenting a model of friendship that is desirable.

## More than a Servant: a Friend

The key reference that Jesus made to friendship is also a key verse used to develop the theme of "servant leadership." Because of the existing emphasis on "servant leadership" in the church and society, I think it's important to look at how Jesus' leadership went beyond "servant-leadership," by identifying his disciples as friends. Earlier, I mentioned John 15:13–16, a passage in which Jesus specifically says, "I no longer call you servants, because a servant does not know his master's business. Instead, I have called you friends, for everything that I learned from my Father I have made known to you."

A great deal has been written on the importance on servant leadership. Jesus taught "servant leadership" and there is no doubt that serving people is important. A "servant leader" understands that ministry requires a leader to humbly serve others in order to obediently express God's love in this world. The servant leader model is different from hierarchical models. It is a model where all leaders are willing to do menial tasks when necessary, to assume the kind of humble leadership personified in Jesus. A key passage that this model is based on is Mark 10:42–45:

> Jesus called them together and said, 'You know that those who are regarded as rulers of the Gentiles lord it over them, and their high officials exercise authority over them. Not so with you. Instead, whoever wants to become great among you must be your servant, and whoever wants to be first must be slave of all. For even the Son

of Man did not come to be served, but to serve and to give his life as a ransom for many."

A servant leader has a high regard for others and a humble view of self. But did Jesus always function in the role of a servant? The "servant leadership" model poses some drawbacks:

1. Being a slave has a negative connotation. Since when did a person really want to give up their freedoms to become a slave? It is true that a "bondservant" (one who willingly gives up their freedom to be a slave for life) is a powerful picture of one's willingness to submit him or herself to the Lordship of Christ. Still, being a servant is rarely the attractive ambition of anyone. Jesus understood this and made this statement knowing that it would be met with resistance.

2. Servants do tasks out of obligation. They have no choice and it is their duty. Consequently, things are done because people have to do them, not necessarily because they want to. The role of the servant leader will compel one to action in order to fulfill their duty as a servant.

3. Servants lack ownership of the cause that they serve. Because they are servants, they do not have a personal sense of responsibility for the big picture. They are just doing what has been commanded. Did Jesus call all to be servants? Yes. Was Jesus a servant? Yes. But does he call his followers to remain exclusively in a servant role, at all times? No. In many ways, friends fulfill the role of a servant without identifying themselves as servants. It is a natural characteristic of friendship. A leader who leads as a friend fulfills the qualities of a servant, but does so with a different motivation. A friend focuses more on the other person and the relationship than on the task.

Instead of viewing his disciples as servants, he called them friends. A relationship of friendship is drastically different than a relationship of servitude. Friendship includes compassion and caring; it involves the heart. It is a relationship that includes the expression of love in a committed relationship. A friend will willingly drop everything to visit a friend that is in the hospital. A leader can serve and not have friendship, but rarely is there a friend who does not serve. Serving can be approached as a job description or a list of duties to be fulfilled. Friends do things for each other, not because they must, but because they want to. It is a relationship of choice, not regulated by formal obligations. For these reasons, it becomes clear that "servant leadership" is not the ultimate posture for a leader who sees the ministry of Jesus Christ as their leadership model. In fact, Jesus' example shows us how leadership relationships evolve and mature. "Friendship leadership" is a term that more aptly describes the state of the relationship between Jesus and his disciples at the end of his earthly ministry.

## The Book of Acts

Jesus developed friendships with the disciples that would be carried on even when he was no longer present in the flesh. In fact, Jesus prepared the disciples for an ongoing friendship with God that would be possible through the Holy Spirit after his death and resurrection. The Holy Spirit would be to them all that Jesus had been during his time on earth. "Jesus promised them that rather than ending his relationship with them, there would be a deepening of it."[10]

The Holy Spirit makes this transforming friendship available to Christians today. Weatherhead writes:

> If Jesus constantly appeared to us now, not only, I am afraid, should we be incredulous, but we should tend to think of the friendship as existing on the shallower levels of intercourse, whereas, as we have seen, the deepest friendships of all are those which function in the unseen parts of the personalities; and God, unseen, inaudible, and intangible, and only so, can enter into His own secret dwelling within us of which He alone has the key.[11]

It is through this relationship with the Holy Spirit that friendship with Christ was bridged in the post-resurrection era.

The book of Acts is a story of networks of friends who form teams and spread the Gospel from place to place. Through these stories, the concept of Friendship Leadership is given form. The disciples continued to live out the new way of interacting they had learned from Jesus: influencing others through friendship. Let the following examples spark your creative understanding of the relational dynamics:

10. Houston, *The Transforming Friendship*, 138.

11. Weatherhead, *The Transforming Friendship*, 65-66.

*Barnabas and Paul:*

One of the essential elements of friendship is the drawing out of identity, which is exactly what Barnabas did for Paul. When Paul first arrived on the ministerial scene, he was newly-converted and full of passion. Yet, perhaps justifiably, everyone was suspicious of this former-persecutor—everyone, except Barnabas. A man of good standing and reputation in the Christian community, Barnabas saw in Paul a true and humble heart. Instead of fretting about his reputation or hiding behind his credentials, he used those tools to vouch for Paul, opening a door of opportunity for him that Paul couldn't open himself (Acts 9:27). It was a kind gesture, but it was only the beginning of a years-long friendship.

After Paul had been sent away for his own safety, he was never far from Barnabas' mind. Barnabas had moved onto Antioch, and was experiencing great success in his ministry there. But Barnabas knew this wasn't the only goal of ministry. So he interrupted his work to travel to Tarsus, specifically to find Paul and bring him back to Antioch, where they worked alongside each other for a year. And over the subsequent years and countless adventures, their relationship moved deeper, from mentorship to friendship. This shift becomes evident as their disagreements are noted, yet still are solved in time.

It's worth observing that Barnabas made a habit of Friendship Leadership, extending it to John, Mark, and Timothy. Barnabas exemplifies an encourager, one who walks alongside other leaders. Beyond formal training, Barnabas lived his life with others, allowing his friendship to shape his ministry and those with whom he ministered.

*Paul and Priscilla and Aquila:*

Sometimes friendship flows from shared beliefs; other times, it begins with just a common interest. For Priscilla and Aquila, they found a friend in Paul through their common business of tent-making. They recently had been exiled from Rome, as Jews had been marked for deportation at the edict of Emperor Claudius. If anyone could use a friend, it was mostly likely these two, who had lost their home and settled in Corinth. When Paul arrived in town, he heard about their tent-making business and sought them out for that reason, living and working with them for some time. Over the course of their time with Paul, both Priscilla and Aquila became followers of the way. When it was time for Paul to leave, they went with him. And when they had to part ways, Paul continued to send his love and greetings to them specifically (Rom 16:3; 2 Tim 4:19), and sending greetings from them in his letter back to the Corinthians (1 Cor 16:19). It is obvious that the time they spent living and working together developed a keen friendship of encouragement.

## Other Examples

Paul, Silas and Timothy all spent considerable amounts of time traveling together, establishing churches and preaching the Gospel. While traveling, they often stayed in homes, sharing meals and life. Through friendship, Paul influenced Philemon on behalf of Onesimus. References are found in Acts to the friends who protected Paul and provided for him during his missionary journeys. This demonstrates the critical support that friendship can provide.

The extensive greetings found in the Epistles reveal vast networks of friends that the apostles had with the leaders of the early church. Romans 16 and First Corinthians 16 contain two of the more extensive lists of greetings, and are full of the expressions of love and affection that typify strong friendship. These enduring relationships provided the apostles with the ability to confront and correct in love, without jeopardizing the relationship.

Cornelius engages in friendship evangelism when he gathers his family and friends together to hear the Good News in Acts 10:24.41. "Friendship evangelism" is a highly effective form of evangelism. This is due to the ability of friends to influence (or lead) in ways inaccessible through other means of relationship.

The pivotal role of friendship in the life of a leader is an expression of the fact that God works through people. The closer people are in relationship, the greater the opportunity exists for them to be influenced by those relationships. God uses friendship as an opportunity to influence, encourage, correct, advise, teach, and comfort.

Friendship with God is a clear theme throughout Scripture. It is an expression of the work of redemption in the life of every believer. Scripture itself clearly calls all followers of Christ not only to receive friendship with God, but also to extend friendship to others. This is a distinct and vital element in Christian leadership.

## Snapshots of Friendship Leadership in Church History

Although I cannot give an overview of church history in this section, I would like to present two different pictures of Friendship Leadership from the time of the early monastic communities and late nineteenth century Christianity.

### Monastic Communities: Scholastica and Benedict

Not long after our accounts from the New Testament draw to a close, our church history tells of men and women who retreated into the desert, seeking a life of sacrifice in pursuit of holy living. Solitude was the aim, but was often interrupted by the draw of relationship. From the Egyptian desert father, Anthony, to the Italian twins, Benedict and Scholastica, these intended hermits ultimately attracted others into their realm of influence. Though they did not pursue this level of community involvement or exposure, it was the result of living with wisdom and integrity; in short, they were leaders. As people drew around each of these figures, the need arose to develop a code of living, a "rule," so to speak. One of these eventually developed into the Rule of St. Benedict: a code of living still followed today by Benedictine monks and nuns fifteen centuries later. It outlined how each of these communities should live together as family and friends.

About life as a nun in the Benedictine order, one ministry writes: "In many ways, we are family. We go out for our ministries, but return in the evening for meals, conversation and leisure activities together. On any evening, you might see Sisters piecing together jigsaw puzzles, playing Scrabble, strolling around the lake or watching TV together. We are here for one another, always."[12]

Sr. Marlene says,

> There is a lot of give and take, and the intergenerational dynamic is similar. Our monastic profession reflects our commitment to community. We promise to be faithful and committed. We promise to accept life's changes and to deepen our relationship with God and each other in so doing. And, we promise obedience, which doesn't mean we give up our own wills or blindly obey. To obey means to listen, and to honor the needs of others in community. It's a matter of maturity: to go to choir practice at the appointed time; to attend

---

12. "Our Life," *Sisters of St. Benedict St. Mary Monastery.*

the meetings you're requested to attend; to do your part as a community member every day.[13]

The friendship of community-living enriches and deepens this tradition of religious leadership. Life is experienced together as each member of the community walks alongside the others, providing encouragement and accountability. Each sister and brother submits to the others, serving them and prioritizing the leadership of others within their life and taking on the role of leader to their friends and co-laborers.

A couple years ago, a friend of mine visited a Benedictine monastery and was treated to one sister's favorite story of the historical Scholastica. It's recorded that the twins, Benedict and Scholastica, each established a monastic community and lived according to the community rule.[14] They ministered and devoted their lives to the work of God. Once a year, these two would reunite to pray together and encourage one another (their version of a family reunion).

On one such occasion, late in life, Scholastica and Benedict were enjoying their time together when evening fell. Benedict's Rule indicated that he was not able to pass the night outside his monastery, so Benedict gathered his things and rose to leave. Scholastica, on the other hand, wasn't ready to say goodbye. She treasured her time with her twin brother, and wanted to continue praying and worshiping God together. Benedict, focused on his task of returning to his cloistered rooms, refused her request. (I get the sense that both siblings were a little stubborn, don't you?) According to the story, at this point, Scholastica bowed her head in prayer. Outside, from a clear sky, a wild storm appeared out of nowhere, lashing wind and rain against the humble cottage in which they were having dinner. Unable to leave the house in the tempest, Benedict was frustrated—through her prayer, she had completely upset his plan. Now, he was going to have to break his own rule. As the thunder rolled and lightning flashed, he turned to his sister and cried, "What have you done?"

She responded, "I asked a favor from you, and you said, 'no.' So I asked God, and he said, 'yes.'"

Knowing he couldn't venture out into the storm, Benedict settled back down into the cottage, and they spent the rest of the evening in prayer and

---

13. "Our Life," *Sisters of St. Benedict St. Mary Monastery.*

14. The Order of St. Benedict, "CHAPTER THIRTY-THREE: OF A MIRCALE WROUGHT BY HIS SISTER SCHOLASTICA."

worship. It would be the last time the twins saw each other; Scholastica died three days later.

This story is also recorded in the Dialogues of Pope Gregory the Great.[15]

At the end of the story, Gregory writes that the wishes of Scholastica were heeded over the wishes of Benedict by God because she "recognized that 'God is love.'" As there was more love in her desire to deepen her friendship with her twin brother than in his desire to follow his rule, God granted her request. Pope Gregory summarized it like this: "Therefore, as is right, she [Scholastica] who loved more, did more."

The nun recounted the story to my friend as an example of the values of monastic communal living: though they live by rules, those rules are submitted to the deep friendship of living life together. The one who loves more, does more.

## Nineteenth-Century Christianity: Thomas and Charles

How many friendships begin with one man burning another man's sermons? Not too many, I would guess. And yet, the unlikely connection between Thomas Johnson and Charles Spurgeon began at that moment, as Thomas, a Southern slave of twenty-eight years, was forced by his master (and a local preacher) to throw the abolitionist writings of Charles into a roaring bonfire. But as he watched the flames devour the text, Thomas knew in his secret heart that Charles was special and thanked God for the preacher "who had the audacity to confront slavery from the other side of the world."[16]

In their recent book, *Steal Away Home: Charles Spurgeon and Thomas Johnson, Unlikely Friends on the Passage to Freedom*, authors Matt Carter and Aaron Ivey present the story of the individual histories and subsequent friendship of these two figures in history. Though I will present a brief picture of their friendship here, I would recommend reading through the entire book.

Thomas and Charles couldn't have been more oppositely situated in life. One, a freed slave from the plantations that once ruled the South, and the other, a celebrated preacher from a small rural community in England.

15. The Order of St. Benedict, "CHAPTER THIRTY-THREE: OF A MIRCALE WROUGHT BY HIS SISTER SCHOLASTICA."

16. Carter and Ivey, *Steal Away Home*, 141.

Many have heard of Charles Spurgeon, as his sermons and writings dominated the theological scene of the mid-to-late nineteenth century and continue to influence us today (for a long time, my daily devotions included *Morning and Evening*).

Brought up in a loving Christian home with a profound awareness of God's presence in his life, Charles knew his life was ordained for ministry and leadership. Over the years, his ministry flourished as he spoke on behalf of the hurting and the hopeless. By the age of nineteen, his weekend congregation surpassed 4,000 people; not long after that, it reached 20,000. His wedding graced the front pages of newspapers, and his literature was printed and distributed worldwide. He was a celebrity (even notorious in places like the South, where his anti-slavery writing earned him the honor of his own book-burnings, like the one mentioned before).

Not many knew, however, how deeply Charles struggled with his own doubts and fears. In addition to constant physical pain (a result of chronic gout), he suffered through ongoing depression and anxiety. A shadow had hovered over him since childhood, and no amount of ministerial success could diminish it. Beneath the exterior of fruitful ministry was a man who could use a friend.

Across the ocean, Thomas Johnson was raised under the cruel tyranny of slavery. He never knew his father, and his mother was heartlessly torn away from him while he was still a child. From that day on, as he worked in backbreaking toil, he dreamed of freedom. Just at the point when he could not endure the hopelessness any longer, he met Jesus, and in that meeting, he felt he found true freedom. Under the cover of darkness, a small group of God's enslaved beloved gathered in a shack after a torturous day of labor, whispering their prayers and worship. This was Thomas' church for many years. Though he had dwindling hope for physical freedom, he found freedom in Jesus.

When the war ended, Thomas found his joy in telling others about the freedom to be found in God, thus beginning his career as a minister. He began in Chicago, but felt a call to return to Africa, and to bring the Good News with him. For this reason, he was recommended to a Bible school founded by—you guessed it—Charles Spurgeon, the very pastor whose literature he had burned all those years before. Upon hearing of Thomas' application to the school, and need for a full scholarship, Charles wrote: "Let the dear man come."

As the founder of the Bible college and pastor of thousands, Charles could have hidden behind the title and position. Fear of intimacy, fear of the unknown and fear of rejection work as stumbling blocks in many relationships. But theirs was an exceptional relationship, as the very first meeting included the shedding of many tears, the revealing of deep wounds, and the tenderness of connected souls. In that quiet meeting space, Thomas ministered to Charles, the "Prince of Preachers."

Through their friendship, Thomas learned many things from the experienced pastor, and Charles' experience with Thomas was described: "For years, he [Charles] had been the answer-giver, the sage who poured out all the answers—sometimes, as if he had learned them all by rote. But, for the first time in a long time, Charles felt like he was being seen, for when Thomas saw him, he saw the *real* Charles—full of pain, sorrow, suffering, and grief."[17]

This is the way their friendship began: humbly and honestly. Thomas Johnson and Charles Spurgeon began their friendship in 1876, in the quiet questions of middle age and grief, despair, and endurance. Both shared a passion for freedom, and the brokenness that accompanies tortured bodies and hearts. In all this, their friendship became a catalyst for mutual hope and faith. They committed themselves to each other, and remained true to that friendship for the rest of their lives.

For more about their friendship, again I would encourage you to read the whole book. But I leave you with this quote from the authors: "Charles also found that brotherly friendships were a powerful force in the war against darkness, and when Sabbath rest was paired with the company of a beloved friend, the days were brighter indeed. One of those beloved friends quickly became Thomas Johnson."[18]

I hope these selected stories from throughout the expansive narrative of our communal Christian journey have demonstrated to you the consistency of Friendship Leadership. It has been present since the very beginning with our Creator-God, and continues today with the Holy Spirit, extending friendship to us and breathing into our relationships with each other. In the next section, we will give a closer look to the definition and description of Friendship Leadership.

17. Carter and Ivey, *Steal Away Home*, 223. Emphasis added.

18. Carter and Ivey, *Steal Away Home*, 186.

# PART 2

Practicing Friendship Leadership

3

## Friendship Leadership Defined

As another lengthy leadership conference for pastors neared its end, I found my attention and retention capacities had been surpassed long ago. In that mid-conference mind haze, I was still clear on this important detail: one block away from the convention center stood the Pepsi Center–the home ice for the Colorado Avalanche hockey team—and that evening they were going to be playing my favorite NHL team: the Vancouver Canucks.

My friend Jerry (you met him in the Introduction) attended the conference with me, and I mentioned the upcoming game to him, revealing I had never been to an NHL game in person. I looked up to Jerry as a leader in my life; he was a well-published author, a faithful pastor and frequently a keynote speaker at this same annual conference we were attending. So you can imagine my surprise and delight when, upon hearing this information, Jerry smiled with excitement and exclaimed, "Let's get tickets and go!" Before I knew it, Jerry had purchased two of the last remaining seats and were on our way to the arena.

We laughed, we cheered, and our team won the game. Walking back to the convention center, we were all smiles. Jerry and I slipped into the general session at about 9:30 p.m. without making a scene, amazed the speaker was just starting to make his final point. We agreed that the investment in friendship that we had made that evening was far more memorable, impactful and encouraging than another session of conference overload. I knew I was experiencing the joy and the influence of Friendship Leadership.

## Some Working Definitions

### Friendship

Breaking down the meaning of Friendship Leadership requires we examine both components of this process: friendship and leadership. Let's begin with friendship.

As humans, our understanding of friendship is diverse, its many manifestations and definitions reflecting the broad worldwide understanding of this somewhat abstract concept. While many have their own personalized understanding of friendship, I felt it was necessary for the context of this book to describe and define what *I* mean when I write about friendship. For this reason, I would like to begin by looking first at Isaacs' definition from his book, *Toxic Friends, True Friends,* "Friendship is a relationship of voluntary interdependence where two people get together because they want to—and take a personalized interest in (and feel concern for) each other."[1]

Out of that definition, a few specific values jump out at us. These are key elements we can look for when we are determining the nature of friendship:

*Mutuality:* In Isaac's definition, there is the understanding that both people are involved in the process of establishing the relationship. A one-sided relationship may be many things, but friendship is not one of them.

Have you ever been in a friendship, only to discover you were the *only one* in the friendship? That your supposed friend didn't see the relationship like that, at all? Or perhaps you've experienced the reverse—you realized that someone had been considering *you* a friend, unbeknownst to you? As someone who has witnessed both of these scenarios, I emphasize the mutuality of friendship. *Both* people need to know that they're in the friendship, and both people need to choose to be there, which leads to,

*Volition:* This definition also speaks of the voluntary choice that undergirds friendship. In order for friendship to remain pure in motivation, each must choose to build the relationship not out of obligation, duty, or simply to be a more effective leader, but out of love. We'll discuss motivation at greater lengths later, but for now, it's safe to say if a relationship is built upon selfish gain, coercion, or false feelings, then it can't be classified as friendship.

*Interdependence:* Friendship should include both people choosing a state of interdependence as a means of establishing trust and building

1. Isaacs, *Toxic Friends, True Friends,* 210.

vulnerability. At times, this can seem counter-cultural, especially in parts of the world where independence is a highly-valued trait. Some even reject it outright as a sign of weakness. But mutual interdependence is a vital life-giving element within relationships between Christians, who relate as members of the Body of Christ. We can get a sense of what this healthy interdependence looks like when we read First Corinthians 12:

> How strange a body would be if it had only one part! Yes, there are many parts, but only one body. The eye can never say to the hand, "I don't need you." The head can't say to the feet, "I don't need you" (19–21).

And further in the passage:

> This makes for harmony among the members, so that all the members care for each other. If one part suffers, all the parts suffer with it, and if one part is honored, all the parts are glad. All of you together are Christ's body, and each of you is a part of it (25–27).

If our friendships are to reflect the biblical example, then they should demonstrate a healthy level of interdependence.

*Care*: Finally, the selfless nature of friendship is demonstrated as we act in love, turning our eyes off ourselves and onto each other. Supportive action will be the natural consequence of the caring connection we make. Feelings, though intrinsic to friendship, should always be coupled with tangible expressions of care.

Through Isaacs' definition, we know to look for the elements of mutuality, volition, interdependence, and care. Building upon this definition, we will now look at the language used in the Bible to define friendship.

## In the Greek

The words and language we use generally have a narrative attached to them, whether it be feelings or inherent understandings passed down through the generations. When we want to grasp just how we reached a certain common understanding of a particular idea or concept (like friendship), going back to the root words is often helpful for creating a more complete picture of its essence. In other words, don't skip this part. (Even if it *is* all Greek to you. Sorry, bad joke.)

As mentioned before, the Greek word for friend is φίλος (pronounced: *philos*). We find examples of this word being used in the New Testament, often describing an associate or a companion. Jesus himself uses this word three times in John 15:13–15: "Greater love has no one than this, that he lay down his life for his *friends*. You are my *friends* if you do what I command. I no longer call you servants, because a servant does not know his master's business. Instead, I have called you *friends*, for everything that I learned from my Father I have made known to you."

Although I added the italicized emphasis, Jesus' repetition of the word draws the attention of his disciples to the nature of their relationship as he saw it, allowing the inherent recognition of language and word choice to guide their understanding.

Friendship was the progressive outcome of Jesus' relationship with the disciples. A servant-master relationship had changed into a bond of friendship. While Jesus didn't explicitly offer his definition of friendship, three key elements implicitly shaped these relationships:

*Love:* Jesus established and maintained his friendships with the disciples through obedience to the command to "love one another." We see love existed as a necessary ingredient for the successful friendships Jesus inhabited. Breaking down "love" to its root, the biblical authors used the Greek word αγάπη (pronounced: *agapé*) to describe the love that would have characterized these friendships. *Agapé* love, understood to be 'divine and unconditional love,' is the love that makes friendships strong, sustainable and lasting.

Within Christian friendship, the behavior and expression of Christian character is revealed in the presence of *agapé*. It binds one person to another, a covenant that the love will remain even through hurt and failure. Love does not depend on performance. As we read about biblical descriptions of friendship, it becomes clear that these two facets of relationship—friendship and love—go hand-in-hand, as we saw in the previous chapters. This passage, specifically, demonstrates that Scripture does not describe friends or friendship by making a distinction between *agapé* and the "love of friends;" they are inextricable. As we move forward building our understanding of friendship, we, too, should avoid trying to make such distinctions. Biblical friendship does not exist without the sharing of *agapé* love.

*Sacrifice:* The expression of *agapé* in Christian friendship includes a sacrificial element. The reference that Jesus makes in the above passage to willingly lay one's life down for a friend reveals the way friendship is not self-serving. Friendship must not become a way to achieve one's own goals. While this may seem like an obvious element of friendship, this becomes increasingly important (and harder to monitor) as we add it to the context of leadership. It contrasts the self-serving methodology of many leaders, and could be described as the junction point between "servant leadership" and "friendship leadership." A friend recently shared her experience re-evaluating what sacrifice meant in her context of Friendship Leadership:

> I reached a point when I realized I was relying on my friends to make my ministry look good. Every time I needed volunteers for an event or promotion, I would think of how my friends could "plug in." ("It will be good for them," I would tell myself.) And when they turned me down ("busy with kids' soccer," "too tired," "not interested"), I would take it personally. It felt like a rejection of not just my ministry, but of me. As my friends, didn't they want to support me? Didn't they understand that their non-participation in my ministries made me look bad? It was soon after I began having these thoughts that I realized I needed to take a step back. I started making a conscientious effort to focus on them, as my friends. I wouldn't bring up my ministry needs, unless I knew I could do it without needing them to "give back to me." And when my friends did decide to join in any ministry efforts, I began to recognize and appreciate it for what it was: not something they owed me, but a sacrifice on their part that I was humbled to receive.

When we live out biblical friendship, we are aware of and respond to the needs of our friends, even when it may not perfectly align with our goals as leaders. This type of leadership remains others-centric, as opposed to self-centric (Watch out. We sometimes disguise "self-centric" as "mission-centric" or "goal-centric"—we have to keep an honest heart regarding our motivations.) In reality, the people in our lives can sense if we're a leader who, as a friend, *builds up*; or a leader who uses friendship as a means to *take*. The truth of our motivation will always be discovered. And while no motivation is probably ever 100 percent pure (we are human, after all), the effort to draw ourselves deeper into biblical friendship can be evident in our lives, while we offer and receive grace for the journey into the heart of God.

Please note, however, we are not referring to a type of sacrifice that would ignore the boundaries necessary in healthy relationships. Healthy boundaries offer everyone freedom; an unhealthy lack of boundaries will only inhibit true friendship and damage the people involved.

*Disclosure:* Finally, we read that friendship developed between Jesus and his disciples through disclosure. In "making everything known to them," the deepening intimacy changed the dynamics of the relationship from one of servitude to one of friendship. The disciples became friends of Jesus because all that he had heard from the Father, he revealed to them. A Lord or master may keep a great deal of information away from their servants, but Jesus treated the disciples as friends by disclosing "all things" to them. More than information, as our example of perfect friendship, Jesus disclosed himself fully, allowing himself to be fully known. This type of knowing transcends the mere exchange of information; it reveals and welcomes someone else into our inner place of identity. The context in which friendship is described in this passage shows friendship as a relationship with a high level of trust, disclosure, and intimacy.

We are vulnerable when we disclose ourselves to our friends. Vulnerability is not a weakness when we are with people who love us. It will deepen a friendship more quickly than anything else. When I disclose the fact that I have failed, that I am weak, or that I am in pain, true friends stand together. When marriages are struggling, when one's health fails, and when careers feel like dead ends, disclosure becomes a fast lane to strength and intimacy.

I can already imagine some responses: How much can I reveal? How honest can I be? Surely, not *everything*? These questions can bring a leader to a place of self-imposed isolation, which could end up being the greatest cause of their downfall. The truth is that friendship does involve risk, and as a potential barrier to friendship, we'll discuss it more in chapter 7. We also include "disclosure" here, however, as it is intrinsic to the nature of friendship. How can we know and be known if we refuse to reveal who we are? How can we learn what acceptance feels like if we only give people the opportunity to accept our false self or an image we project? Disclosure of who we are, and what we're about, is necessary for true friendship to form.

But this is only half of the Friendship Leadership equation. With these descriptions of friendship in mind, let's pause to look more closely at the values of leadership in this context.

## Leadership

Though many books have focused on the subject of leadership, each with a corresponding definition, in my experience, leadership comes down to purposeful influence. Leaders are individuals who exert either a formal or informal influence on the people around them. This strength of influence makes it possible for a person to lead those around them, even those higher up in the hierarchy. I believe the Bible often encourages us to pursue this type of influence, recognizing that children can set the example in faith, the young can lead the older through lifestyle, and the unschooled can teach the scholars a thing or two. Influence, given by God and stewarded by humans, lays the foundation for leadership.

The other component of leadership is that it needs to lead *somewhere*; there must be a direction, a heading, a purpose. It doesn't matter if the destination is a particular goal, a hoped-for vision, or a relational reality, leaders understand their role in moving other people (and themselves) forward.

I'm sure we've all met that person whose very presence overflows with influence, yet that influence doesn't lead anyone anywhere. A young man comes to mind who attended the youth group I led. From his childhood through his adolescence, everyone would remark on his incredible ability to gather his peers, drawing them to his internal glow. To be honest, I don't even think *he* knew the kind of raw influence he had, the magnetism. But the observations of his unrefined leadership were always followed by: "It sure is a shame that he doesn't use his influence for anything good." In the end, he ended up spending quite a few years in jail for numerous illegal choices, and the sad thing was that he brought others with him. He had the influence; he just didn't have the direction. Though this serves as a more dramatic example, it reminds me just how important it is for influence to have a purpose.

Taking it one step further, in the context of biblical leadership, we know we aren't merely serving our purposes, but the purposes of God in this world. As leaders, we are pointing people in the direction of the Way, walking alongside others as we all move toward him. The love that God wants us to share and to express is the ultimate goal of every form of Christian leadership.

## Bringing It All Together

In the following chapters, we will examine the benefits and characteristics of healthy friendships in the context of leadership; but before we do, let's boil all this information down to three definitions we will take with us moving forward (this is the part where you pull out your highlighter.)

*Friendship:* A loving relationship of interdependence freely chosen by both people, built upon trust and self-disclosure, acted upon with care and sacrifice.

Though there are countless definitions of leadership out there, I've always thought of it this way:

*Leadership:* The influence of others towards a greater love of God and people.

Combining those two definitions allows us to put Friendship Leadership into words.

*Friendship Leadership:* A philosophy of leadership that finds its foundation in the innate and intentional qualities of friendship.

I am aware that even these definitions have their limitations, but for the purpose of this leadership principle, I feel they will do. Leadership that transforms both people is rooted in these definitions. It can be pursued and applied in numerous contexts.

# 4

## The Benefits of Friendship Leadership

Two sturdy oaks I mean, which side by side,

Withstand the winter's storm,

And spite of wind and tide,

Grow up the meadow's pride,

For both are strong


Above they barely touch, but undermined

Down to their deepest source,

Admiring you shall find

Their roots are intertwined

Insep'rably.

HENRY DAVID THOREAU[1]


THE JOURNEY OF FRIENDSHIP is a joyous journey. As leaders, we can embrace the benefits of this journey, not having to choose between a life of leadership and a life of friendship. Aelred de Rievaulx, the twelfth century saint who wrote the book *Spiritual Friendship* says, "In friendship eternity blossoms, truth shines forth, and charity grows sweet."[2] Aristotle

1. Thoreau, *Friendship*.
2. Keaton, "Friendship as Communion with God," 35.

expressed some of the benefits that friendship brings to people in all stages of life: "The young need it to keep them from error. The old need it to care for them and support the actions that fail because of weakness. Those in their prime need it, to do fine action."[3] Friends are "together when they are separated, they are rich when they are poor, strong when they are weak, and—something even harder to explain—they live on after they have died, so great is the honor that follows them, so vivid the memory, so poignant the sorrow."[4] There are incalculable benefits to allowing deep and vulnerable relationships to take root and grow up strong. Here are just a few of those benefits:

## Spiritual Growth

According to author John Crossin, "Friendships are the key to our spiritual growth." [5] They can correct, encourage, and advise with great authority. Friendships assist in making wise decisions, help with sound judgment, and give us perspective and experience outside and beyond ourselves. It is helpful to talk things over with a friend. I turn to my friends to provide a balance, both encouraging the person I am and advocating for the person they know God is developing in me.

"Good friendships in solid communities are absolutely necessary for us to come to spiritual maturity."[6] They will be there when we go through sickness, conflict, and trial; it is an essential component to the nature of friendship. Friends would do nothing less. Standing shoulder to shoulder with a friend is a tremendous source of strength when faced with difficulty and adversity. It brings about courage, boldness, and accountability in the face of temptation. "People who get along best in life and deal with uncertainties and trials and tribulations have friends," says Alan Booth, PhD, Professor of Sociology and Human Development at Penn State University.[7] A friend would not be true if they did otherwise, so these are not the obligations of friendship, but the byproduct of *phileo* love. If spiritual growth

---

3. Pakaluk, *Other Selves*, 30.

4. Pakaluk, *Other Selves*, 30.

5. Crossin, *Friendship*, 1.

6. Wuthnow, *Sharing the Journey*, 37.

7. Isaacs, *Toxic Friends, True Friends*, 1.

is part of your vision for the future of your leadership, bring true friends alongside—you need them

## Companionship

Friendship is a gift from God, containing the potential to produce a deep satisfaction to the heart. It helps meet our personal needs for companionship and intimacy. Loneliness is satisfied and the quality of one's life is enriched. Because of these great personal benefits, this kind of love must be nurtured, valued, and protected. It must be a point of prayer and is a part of vital spiritual living. Discovering a person who shares an interest, thought, philosophy, or passion can create powerful synergy. This can be directed in a negative or a positive direction. Either way, it is a powerful force, which gives vision a dynamic element that can further passion, courage, sacrifice, and devotion.

## Productivity

Aristotle pointed out that friendship usually arises for the purpose of either personal pleasure or "utility."[8] He makes a distinction between pleasant friends and useful friends—both being valid and important, but also being clearly distinct types of friendships. According to Aristotle, friendships of "utility" are the kinds of friendships that are more conditional, whereas the best kinds of friendship are unconditional. Friendships of "pleasure" are those that one enjoys through shared experience. "Utility" is used to describe the greater industriousness and productivity that comes from working with a friend to accomplish a common task. Both the benefits of companionship and productivity continue to be primary in friendships today. Greater productivity can be expected by leaders who assimilate friendship into their leadership style. But the pleasure of companionship often coincides with the productivity, allowing for transformation and cohesiveness.

8. Pakaluk, *Other Selves,* 34.

## Influence

Leadership seminars are a common part of business and church life today. In these seminars, leaders seek ways of increasing their ability to influence people and organizations. Training and ongoing education provide workers with updated methods in leadership and business. Yet much of this information is never applied. Most people identify key leaders as the strongest influencers in their lives, surpassing information acquisition or education. The attraction of seminars often has more to do with relationships than it does with the seminar content. Seminars and classes rarely impact a person's leadership development as much as friends and mentors do. The same thing is true with books (even this one)—this book will never influence you to the same extent that a key relationship will, and I rejoice in that. People are influenced by other people, and friendships make influence much more relevant and attainable.

Black describes the dynamic aspect of friendship's power in influence:

> Have we put on his armor and sent him out with courage and strength to the battle? Or have we dragged him down from the heights to which he once aspired? In all friendship, we open the gates of the city, and those who have entered must be either allies in the fight or treacherous foes. All the fruits of friendship, be they blessed or baneful, spring from this root of influence, and influence in the long run is the impress of our real character on other lives.[9]

Through influence found in friendship, we not only shape the lives of those around us but the very success of all our hopes and visions lies in the wake of such relationships.

In the research I conducted I found that friendship within a relationship is directly related to the degree of influence that relationship has. Friends have a greater shaping influence on people than positional leaders. "The realization of any friendship means the realization of power. If two people become real friends, then, in the respects in which one is strong and the other admires that strength, that strength, through communion, will pass to the weaker."[10]

Those in our lives are looking for approachable, relational, caring leaders. For this reason, leaders should not excuse themselves from the

9. Black, *The Art of Being a Good Friend*, 48.
10. Weatherhead, *The Transforming Friendship*, 95.

possibility of having friends among their subordinates. People tend to gain respect for leaders when they get to know them personally.

The risks of having friends among those we lead can be successfully managed and will create an environment of spiritual growth, companionship, productivity, and increased influence. When friendships merge, a great environment for learning, development, and mentoring is created. "The most successful leaders are those who are the most skilled at forging strong, trusting relationships. Constructive, productive relationships are the bedrock of every organization that wished to be more than an overnight, short-lived success."[11]

The benefits of Friendship Leadership are felt both in the immediate and in the eternal.

## Loving Expression

Friendship Leadership provides the space for caring relationships to take place, allowing the expressions of selfless love to flourish. For me, as a Christian leader, this is perhaps the greatest benefit of the philosophy. Care, as it is expressed by Christian leaders, is essential as an ethical prerogative that can be fulfilled through friendship. The risks involved in friendship are real, but they yield to the biblical mandate to love, and the model of Christ who led his disciples through friendship. Christian leaders have a moral responsibility to care for people deeply, not merely exercise positional leadership skills. Techniques for organizational success can be applied by any leader, but from God's vantage point, without love, our work amounts to nothing (1 Cor 13).

Leadership books provide readers with formulae promising that if certain techniques are implemented, certain outcomes will take place. But while leadership skills may be helpful to know as a leader, when they are applied without heart, without relational investment, followers are often resentful because they are reduced to the role of human "resources," or worse, cogs in a machine. By themselves, leadership techniques when applied can be dehumanizing. They can leave the followers feeling empty and possibly even used.

The truth is that a friend occupies a special space unreachable by the professional. During a time of personal crisis, a pastor who makes a mandatory "house call" functions very differently than a friend who responds to

11. Tracy and Morin, *Truth, Trust, and the Bottom Line*, 22.

the same situation. Who is functioning more *pastorally*? Who is more *caring*? Professionals do have something to offer; their expertise, understanding, and outside perspective can all be of critical importance to people who are going through a crisis. But it also reinforces a hierarchical dependency, because the professional comes in as an expert who is being paid for their services. Although they may genuinely care for the people they respond to, they are fulfilling a professional role that may also be an obligation of that role, whereas a friend will intervene and care voluntarily.

With friendship, the levels of care and empathy go way up. A leader with positional authority who understands these dynamics can approach a crisis as an opportunity to exercise friendship, sincerity, and the expression of authentic care. If a leader fails to approach people with the level of care with which they would treat a friend, they will easily revert to using people to accomplish goals, regardless of the personal impact it has on the followers. This kind of hierarchical leadership does not care for followers at a personal level. It values results and self-interest more than anything else.

Resisting this temptation, Christian leaders should be encouraged to think of others more than themselves. To use people without any regard for who they are as human beings blatantly violates scripture. *Christians are called to love.* Scripturally, love and friendship are often used synonymously. Leadership that embraces people as friends cultivates a sense of belonging and directs people toward God's love. Love is non-negotiable. Friendship Leadership benefits us as it provides us with a framework for expressing that love.

It is difficult to love people without being open to friendship. Friendship and love are tightly intertwined, as we observed in the biblical use of *agapé* in the last chapter. The absence of love in leadership compromises a Christian leader's ability to be eternally effective. To ignore "the greatest commandment" by saying, "It doesn't belong in the workplace," or, "It doesn't apply," in whatever situation a leader finds him or herself in, is obviously wrong. By excusing themselves from love, many Christian organizations have developed a reputation for being no better than worldly institutions, and Christian leaders no more compassionate or moral that their secular counterparts.

To befriend someone, surprisingly, is not necessarily more demanding than fulfilling a professional expectation. It does mean that a person will approach the situation with a different mindset. It requires more heart, and a greater emotional commitment, but that is part of empathy, quality care, and understanding the heart of God. To care as a friend does not demand that a person "do more"—it is not necessarily about quantitative caring. All people have a limited number of hours in a day, and families, self-care, and other demands all restrict the amount of time that can be given in any situation. But time does not have to limit the depth of care, nor the way in which people are thought of or responded to.

Friendship dynamics reveal compassionate behavior that not only exceeds the caring of professionals, but sometimes even that of family. "Friends choose to do what kin are obliged to do."[12] (I can think of many times when, based on the depth of our friendship, I've been invited into a life circumstance of a friend when their family was unable or unwilling to show up.) Though family usually provides stability, consistency, and grace in relationships that is often stronger than in friendships, friends are not obligated to care, which makes the caring of friends distinct from the caring of families. Friendship is unique in that it is a chosen relationship, tied together by the bonds of a unique love and commitment that is based on the relationship itself, and not obligated by blood or professionalism. A person engaged in "intentional friendship" is outward focused. They are not seeking personal happiness and fulfillment. They are interested in having as maximum of an impact as a person can have on another. For them, "caring" is always worth it.

Because friends care more deeply for one another than people fulfilling professional roles, Christian leaders can embrace friendship as they consider how to express love in their leadership. People in crisis are often feeling lonely and are not interested in meeting with another professional who is "doing their job." Instead, they need a friend, and Christians have the calling and the opportunity to meet them in a way that no professional can.

## What Happens Without Friendship?

Some, in reading about Friendship Leadership, may be tempted to think: "Well, that's all well and good for others, but I'll pass just the same." But, bringing friendship into our leadership is not just beneficial, the *absence* of friendship in leadership can be detrimental. C.S. Lewis, in contemplating such as absence of friendship, wrote, "As long as each of these percipient

---

12. Rubin, *Just Friends*, 39.

persons dies without finding a kindred soul, nothing (I suspect) will come of it; art or sport or spiritual religion will not be born." [13]

In making this statement, Lewis is expressing the fact that friendship brings about higher expressions of life and lasting influence. In the absence of friendship, creativity is lessened, production decreases, and a willingness to take risks is compromised. Shared experiences are powerful and have a greater impact on all who are involved.

The following dangers exist when friendship is not valued:

1. *In the absence of friendship, isolation is dominant.*

   The isolation of leaders is one of the greatest dangers to any organization. It puts the leader and the organization in a precarious place, where ethics can be compromised, and the vacuum of information leads to a skewed perception of reality. Unfortunately, pastors are some of the most isolated people in our society. Lacking friends and unsure of whom to trust, their leadership and effectiveness will be short-circuited. The cultural adage, "It gets lonely at the top," expresses a pull that every leader faces. It is a pull toward isolation. It is a pull that comes from demands on time, expectations, and misplaced priority. Pastors and church leaders also have been taught not to get too close to people, and people generally see them through a stain-glassed lens which creates the impression of unapproachability.

   > The greater the degree of influence, the greater the potential for a leader to lead a lonely and hidden existence, where people only see what the leader wants them to see. As leaders increase in stature, a significant temptation draws them like a magnet. They are seduced into hiding the truth about themselves in order to create or maintain an image that they believe will maintain their influence. Many environments discourage vulnerability. [14]

   The authors of *The Ascent of a Leader* warn against this danger, and encourage leaders to choose vulnerability in order to enhance integrity and to ultimately be more effective.

2. *Without friendship, our ability to experience life-transforming change personally, and to have a lasting change on others, is compromised.*

   David Benner states that our progress in personal growth is dependent on these relationships: "If you are making significant progress

13. Lewis, *The Four Loves*, 65.
14. Thrall, *The Ascent of a Leader*, 85.

on the transformational journey of Christian spirituality, you have one or more friendships that support that journey. If you do not, you are not. It is that simple." [15]

This would imply that having a transformational impact on others would also depend on having friendships that would likewise create this opportunity.

3. *Without friendship, turnover is greater, work is arduous, creativity is lessened, and risk is minimized.*

People tend to risk more when they are with friends. Our relationships can provide encouragement and an emotional "safety net." We feel secure knowing that even if our ideas don't always work out the way we want them to, we have friendships of unconditional love keeping us grounded and growing. The people who know us best have the best opportunities to spur us on toward the values, goals, and dreams they know are important to us. As leaders, we can offer our friends the space to be creative, to take risks, to try. We cheer together when the risk pays off, and encourage each other when it doesn't. No matter what, when we have friends within our leadership relationships, we will willingly embrace great challenges that we otherwise would not attempt.

4. *Without friendship, work becomes strictly institutional and about the bottom line.*

People become clients. Employees become pawns used to accomplish organizational goals. Embracing intentional friendships as leaders, in any context, is realizing that the future is dependent on strengthening, changing, or adding relationships. Benner reminds us that the "objectification of people is the heritage of the professionalization of helping relationships . . . When we treat others as objects, even for benevolent reasons, we rob them of their humanity . . . This allows them to relate to them as objects of their professional expertise and avoid personal involvement."[16]

This "professionalization" has been embraced by Christian leaders, taught in classes on caring, and created an appearance of intimacy that is hollow. In some ways, this trend towards professionalization

15. Benner, *Sacred Companions*, 16.
16. Benner, *Sacred Companions*, 55.

has reduced pastoral care and pastoral leadership to techniques to be applied.

Without friendship, without a deep and meaningful relationship, we can also fall into this modern trend. Instead, we need to look for key people with whom we can build a dynamic friendship. If we feel our organization is getting too institutional, cold, and impersonal, we can change that by cultivating personal and caring involvement. This will have a more dynamic effect to turn things around than continuing merely to revise policies.

5. *Without friendship, entire dimensions of life that God created people to enjoy, will be missed.*

These joys include loving and being loved, the joy of sharing common experiences, and the benefit of having people walk alongside each of us through our successes and failures. Without friendship, loneliness grows, along with an unhealthy egoism accentuating the isolation. In the Church, we understand the significance of communion—so why would we, as Christian leaders, eliminate communion from our leadership practices?

6. *Without friendship, spiritual growth stagnates.*

As I mentioned before, spiritual growth is a benefit of friendship; conversely, our spiritual growth has no room to flourish in a life devoid of meaningful friendships.

"A spiritual friend is therefore needed, to awaken my heart out of the sleep of conventionalized, institutionalized, professional ways of our 'normal existence,' to so individuate me that I can take the first serious step in personal prayer." [17]

Friendship compliments our personal contemplative spiritual practices, providing the place where we practice what we've read and heard from our greatest Friend.

7. *Without friendship, life is difficult.*

People were created for relationship, and friendship is one of the most rewarding of all relationships. Friends "are a way for us to be recognized as unique people, to be reassured that we are appreciated for who we are . . . The fact that they are voluntary, easier to enter or leave than family, marriage, or professional relationships, reassures us

17. Houston, *The Transforming Friendship*, 46.

that people remain our friends because they genuinely like us, even when we have hurt or disappointed them."[18]

Friends bring joy and meaning to life by fulfilling one of the deepest needs of the human heart. Like Thoreau's "two sturdy oaks," or the "chord of three strands" in Ecclesiastes 4:12, it is easier to thrive in life, and leadership, as we dwell in the presence of friendship.

18. Kusher, *Living a Life That Matters,* 119.

# 5

## Qualities in Friendship Leadership

"I've been with my friends since childhood. I just don't know if I can make more."

"I have all the friends I want."

"People have always found me unapproachable. I've just accepted it as part of my personality."

"I'm not what you'd call a 'people person.'"

"It's hard to make friends. I'm just not sure it's worth the effort."

"For some reason, other people just don't like me."

I have heard the numerous reasons we tend to disregard the very important pursuit of friendship in our lives. Unless you are one of the rare extra-gregarious "people people" with unwavering self-confidence and only positive experiences within friendship, you may have some reservations about your friendship skills. I know I feel this way, at times. However, since the last chapter showed that leadership that incorporates friendship is more effective than leadership that does not, it is important to demonstrate that the skills of friendship can be taught, learned, and applied.

It's been said that *friendships are born, not made.* People holding to this view believe that friendships arise serendipitously, sometimes spontaneously and always, uniquely. But French philosopher Montaigne saw friendship as being closely tied to a decision of the will. He wrote, "Our free will has no product more properly its own than affection and friendship." [1]

Some leaders, by way of their personality, make friends easily. For other leaders, the process of opening up and making friends is a difficult one. Still, counselors and behavioral experts believe, in near unanimous

1. Pakaluk, *Other Selves*, 186.

agreement, that there are teachable skills that can enhance everyone's ability to make and keep friends.

A great deal of research has already been done in the area of friendship development, showing that good relational skills when learned and applied create an environment where friendships thrive. The remarkable success of Dale Carnegie's book, *How to Win Friends and Influence People,* which has now sold over 15 million copies, shows how the skills of friendship are both desirable, and learnable. Similarly, *The Friendship Factor,* written by Alan Loy McGinnis, is another very successful book that is based on premise that a person can learn how to be a better friend. This we do, not as a ploy to further our own agenda, but to productively communicate and demonstrate our very real care.

People can make the choice to become intentional in caring and developing the skills of dynamic friendship. Tim Sanders, former Chief Solutions Officer at *Yahoo!,* describes his tranformation: "My willingness to commit myself to these people openly and firmly helped them understand that I wasn't selling them a bill of goods. I was sharing my heart because I truly cared as much for their success as I cared for my own . . . I became more emotionally open. I hugged people. I was a two-fisted handshaker. I made eye contact. I smiled." [2]

He goes on to argue strongly that compassion is something we can all do, and when intentionally expressed, it will make a difference in your life as well as in the lives of everyone you meet. The ability to be a good friend to others can be learned and applied regardless of a person's personality type. This is good news for people who are afraid of embracing the value of friendship.

In this chapter, I will introduce eight characteristics for strong and healthy friendships: initiative, time, loyalty and commitment, priority, communication, encouragement, respect, and intimacy. Some of these qualities are skills that can be developed. Some are aspects of character that can be enhanced through spiritual growth, sanctification, and with the help of the Holy Spirit. Finally, others are merely choices of the will.

It takes a conscious effort to nurture an authentic interest in others. [3] The common denominator that binds these characteristics together is that they are all available to people who would choose to pursue them. Finding people with whom to share experiences takes initiative, which is not

2. Sanders, *Love is the Killer App,* 148.

3. Engstrom and Larson, *The Fine Art of Friendship,* 29.

only possible—it's very desirable. We all have an equal amount of time in a day to devote to relationships. Loyalty and commitment to another person is a choice, as is the demonstration of priority. Communication skills can be learned. The ability to encourage and affirm others is available to each of us. Respect can be given when one looks at another human and sees their inherent worth before God. Finally, though its risky, even intimacy is a choice. All of these characteristics require patience as relationship turns into a friendship. Aristotle put it this way: "For though the wish for friendship comes quickly, friendship does not. Friendship takes patience, perseverance and consistency." [4]

The working assumption, however, is that we are interested in the intentional formation and strengthening of friendship—this is not a chapter about accidental friendships. I choose to focus on intentional friendships precisely because many leaders are in environments (corporate, societal, organizational, and familial) where friendships in leadership are discouraged. Some leaders have closed themselves off to the possibilities and the benefits that come from investing in the lives of others at a deeper level. But I believe a leader will be more effective through the intentional development of friendships. Please note, however, that the effectiveness of leadership must not become the overriding goal, or else the authenticity of the friendship is lost from the beginning.

Friendship may be characterized by the qualities listed in this chapter, but at the same time, it is an experience more than it is an idea. For friendship to occur, one must be open to the possibility of forming a new friendship before there is a chance of it actually taking place. We cannot always know where a seed of friendship will fall or take root, but we can offer the nourishment of intentional and selfless investment. Are you open to friendship? Are you prepared to hone your skills with intention, so you're ready when the opportunity for friendship arises?

One final piece of good news: friendship is contagious. It's exponential. Good friends encourage others in the skills of friendship by modeling, and by caring. As James Houston writes, "Hopefully then, friendship may become re-instated once more in the renewed quest for genuine humanity."[5]

This will happen as people anticipate opportunities to build bridges of friendship and compassion. Then, seize the opportunities when they come.

---

4. Pakaluk, *Other Selves*, 34.

5. Houston, *Prayer and Spiritual Friendship*, 3–5.

## Qualities of Friendship

While acknowledging the dynamic nature of friendship, certain universal qualities begin to reveal themselves. These qualities do not define friendship, but describe the way it looks in day-to-day life. They are the building blocks we carefully construct upon the foundation of our definition. As you will find, these qualities interact with and are often a direct result of the defined aspects of friendship.

It is also important to note that these qualities of friendship represent *skills*, in that they can be learned. If, as you read this chapter, you feel disheartened to find your friendships lack a certain quality, be encouraged to know that these can be intentionally introduced into an already-formed friendship. A posture of thoughtful reflection can inspire you to deeper revelations about the nature and future of your friendships.

Before I move on to the specific qualities of friendship, I want to return to the concept of *agapé* love. While I mentioned this love in the previous chapter, including it in the definition, I want to mention it again here. I believe that love isn't just another quality of friendship, but that love infuses and provides the foundation for manifestations of friendship. It is the means by which all other qualities exist. It is *through* love and *by* love that anything else is accomplished. It is the source, evident in every action of friendship. Love informs our skills and motivates our growth. Not a single quality would exist in the absence of love. Have I mentioned I think love is important to friendship? We cannot escape the command to love. Love is a decision, and a fruit of the Spirit that is the most essential quality of Christian behavior. People tend to limit their definition of love to an emotion. The kind of love that Jesus challenged us to exercise was volitional, action-oriented, and behavioral.

We may even try to grapple with these concepts—initiative, time, loyalty and commitment, priority, communication, encouragement, respect, and intimacy—in the realm of our limited human understanding. There are indeed helpful books written on these subjects, and I myself will invest further study into each of these qualities. But unless these are undergirded with a selfless, "gift-love"[6] (as C.S. Lewis would term it), they will be poor copies of a divine standard.

In Lewis' gift-love, friendships are "free from the need to be needed." We offer our friendship, and the qualities that color it, selflessly, not as a

6. Lewis, *The Four Loves.*

means to build up the self. We don't give respect because we want it reciprocated, nor do we offer time and demand its return. We don't encourage so that we can have our own egos stroked, nor do we prioritize others in order to be their top priority. Friendship consists more in loving than in being loved. With friendship there is a bond of love, never simply an obligation to love. Before moving forward, let's adjust our reading focus to consider each of these qualities of friendship through the lens of that *agapé* love.

## Initiative

Years later, I still remember the conversation in my office: she was crying and there wasn't anything I could do for her. The truth was, she was the only person who would be able to help herself. A young woman in my church had asked to meet with me so we could discuss something weighing heavy on her heart. Almost as soon as we sat down, she opened up with:

"I'm so lonely. I just don't have friends."

I expressed I was sorry to hear that, and asked why she thought this might be the case.

"I don't know. It's just that . . . no one ever invites me out."

At which point, I asked if she initiated any hang-outs. "Have you invited anyone over? Or maybe out to the movies? Or to grab coffee?"

She let out a frustrated sigh as she responded, "Well, no, but still. Why is everyone ignoring me? Why doesn't anyone think to include me? It's like they don't see me or care that I'm lonely."

She was truly heartbroken, because she viewed her lack of involvement as personal rejection, as opposed to what it really was: a lack of initiative. This may sound harsh, but friendship requires taking initiative. Until she decided to reach out on her own, instead of waiting for someone else to make the first move, she was probably going to remain relationally unfulfilled (she did eventually take that step of faith, and is now enjoying several close friendships.) If I wait for my friends to call me, they might never call. I have sometimes been frustrated by a lack of initiative in my "friends" and family. I eventually had to face the fact that I have to pick up the phone and initiate in order to cultivate deep and meaningful friendship.

Over the years, I have encountered this same mindset in churches and organizations. A person will begin attending the church, and after a few months of complete lack of involvement, complain that the community isn't very welcoming. Usually, these same people avoid the numerous small groups, outreaches, socializing events and volunteering opportunities we offer. Watching this happen countless times has cemented in my mind that *initiative* is truly a fundamental element of friendship.

In his own friendship leadership, Jesus called the disciples to follow him. He was nearly always taking the initiative in his relationship with the disciples. This was the beginning of friendships that changed the world. Likewise, our friendships begin with someone taking the initiative. People must not spend their life waiting for others to invite them in as friends. Emerson wrote on friendship stating, "The only way to have a friend is to be one."[7]

It may seem one sided, but friendships require proactive steps. "You can make more friends in two months by becoming interested in other people than you can in two years by trying to get other people interested in you."[8]

Within my own staff of church leaders, I encourage them to be as proactive as possible. Before and after services, we have a policy of leaders, staff members and pastors intentionally looking for someone new to befriend. It's true that each staff member and pastor cannot offer a deep friendship to every person in our church, but they can take the initiative with a few, setting the example for those few to take the initiative with others.

As leaders, we can't hide behind the excuse of believing we *deserve* to have others always take the initiative with us. That isn't a very Christ-like model; it's self-satisfying and insular. Let's pursue others the way Christ pursues us. And when others do take the initiative with us, let's appreciate that kindness and the effort they are making on our behalf.

I know this can be hard for some personalities. As an introvert myself, initiating conversations with strangers is less than ideal for me. We will cover more of friendship leadership for introverts later in chapter 11, but for now, be assured that there are ways to take initiative without stretching yourself to your breaking point. Self-awareness, boundaries, and a little risk-taking can make initiative possible for the introvert.

As we continue on to the quality of "Time," I encourage you to challenge your friend-making assumptions: What can you offer? Who can you call today (or text/email/meet for coffee)? What has been stopping you? Take some initiative!

7. Emerson and Mumford, *Friendship,* 169.
8. Carnegie, *How to Win Friends and Influence People,* 43.

## Time

I moved around a lot as a kid. My family was in the military, so I became really good at making friends fast. I knew how to take initiative, and this kept me from ever being lonely for long. But as I grew older, I started noticing that I was missing something from these new friendships. It took a while before I could name the thing I lacked: roots. While all my friends had relationships with long, deep roots, the result of years of shared experiences, trials and joys, my friendships just felt transient and shallow. I decided I would start investing myself in developing those roots. Even as I've had to continue moving around, I do a much better job keeping up long-distance friendships, not letting those years go to waste. And when I move somewhere new, I patiently invest time, believing that as good as a friendship may be now, it will be even better in time.

In his book, *Friendship*, Conway reminds us, "Developing friendships is just that—a development, a process."[9]

A great deal of time is needed in order for the qualities that comprise a good friendship to be shared and experienced in a relationship. For this reason, friendships require that people spend time together. Close friends will *want* to spend time together because without the investment of time, friendships do not have the opportunity to grow in depth.

This time investment secures the necessary friendship value of companionship. Good friends tend to have common interests and compatibility that cause them to enjoy being together and through the investment of time in that companionship, creates an atmosphere in which friendship grows. Working together, playing sports, enjoying a hobby, volunteering in a ministry—these all create the opportunity for people to experience companionship which leads to the development of friendship and the nurturing of existing friendships. A broad range of connection points can diversify our friendships, opening doors to new experiences and passions. When hearts join together in fellowship, the seeds of friendship are planted and begin to grow.

But how do we know when it's enough time? When my mom began gardening, she learned a handy saying about perennial plants: "The first year, they sleep. The second year, they creep. The third year, they leap!" And in the case of her garden, it was true. After years of patient tending, weeding, and feeding, everything sprang to life. While I'm not suggesting

---

9. Conway, *Friendship*, 24.

an exact three-year growth cycle for your friendships, I can encourage you to not be disheartened if the development of friendship seems to be slow-going. Believe that nothing is wasted, and that the time you invest now is forming a solid foundation for years to come. Much like a plant that continues to be nurtured, receiving life-giving water and the warmth of the sun, friendships require an unseen investment of faith. The fruit will come in time, sometimes surprising us in the most wonderful ways.

If you recently relocated to a new community, started a new job or began attending a new church—building relationships of depth is going to take time. Some people never stay long enough to experience the power of friendship. They remain "shallow" and they struggle with loneliness, isolation, and social disconnect. For some, those transitions are even mandatory, as is the case for military spouses. In these situations, we can consider the usefulness of technology to connect consistently, though it isn't always "deep." Text message, email, shared photos, and free long-distance calling all can help us stay connected while going about our busy lives. Though I live two states away from my kids, we still find time to call each other every day, just to check in and invest in our long-term, long-distance friendship.

For others, however, the lack of roots is less a work-related demand, and more an indicator of a lack of prioritization of time investment. In my profession, it is common for pastors to only remain in their positions briefly, moving from church to church every few years. This eliminates the possibility of friendship that only comes through the investment of time.

You may agree that time investment is critical to the development of friendship. But *how* we invest that time can be a key determining factor to its success. Our cultural background affects how we perceive and offer time. Sherwood Lingenfelter offers insight to this particular cultural variance in his book *Leading Cross-Culturally: Covenant Relationships for Effective Christian Leadership*, in which he explains the difference between time- and event-orientation. How we fluctuate between these two ends of a cultural spectrum can directly affect how we approach time within friendship.

To summarize his research, a person who is time-oriented will focus heavily on precision within given time constructs. They will want to be "on time" for things, will understand care through a friend's respect of their time, and will expect the world to conform to a time-sensitive method of making commitments. Conversely, an event-oriented friend will prioritize time through the lens of specific situations. They will be more flexible with the way they manage time, will feel less bound by watches/clocks, and will express and receive care through the restructuring of a series of events to reflect the event happening in that moment.

Here's how a conversation between two friends who find themselves on opposites ends of the spectrum may go:

*Friend 1(Highly time-oriented):* Finally, you show up! I've been waiting twenty minutes for you!

*Friend 2 (Highly event-oriented):* I'm so sorry. My sister called, and she was in one of her crises. You know how that goes . . .

*Friend 1:* It seems like this happens every week. Couldn't you have called her back? Or told her we had a coffee date scheduled?

*Friend 2:* I did! But she was crying a lot, and it just seemed best to stay on the phone with her.

*Friend 1:* Well, I have a meeting right after this, so those twenty minutes will have to cut into our coffee date. Hopefully next time, we'll get our full time in.

*Friend 2:* I'm sure it won't happen next week!

Both friends felt justified in how they approached time investment within friendship. *Friend 1* demonstrated love for *Friend 2* by showing up on time for a scheduled appointment and by not allowing the tardiness of *Friend 2* to affect the next appointment. However, a little time buffer in *Friend 1*'s life could alleviate some of the tension. *Friend 2* demonstrated love by prioritizing the pain of the sister over an arbitrary schedule. Yes, in an ideal situation, *Friend 2* would have been on time, but life happens and so they adapted with it to meet the needs of the sister. But in their own way, *Friend 2* could have been more sensitive to *Friend 1*'s tight schedule and communicated better with either *Friend 1* or the sister (at the very least, *Friend 2* could examine whether this was a one-time event, or a recurring pattern in their life.) In both cases, each friend wanted to invest the necessary time into friendship. But this is a reminder to make sure to communicate your time- or event-orientation to those in your life (it could save you some fighting and frustration.) In leadership, we'll work with both kinds of people, so an awareness of this cultural difference will be vital to investing productive time into friendships.

This scenario describes my marriage perfectly. While I have a high time-orientation, my wife is event-oriented. I used to think her tendency to be late was selfish and inconsiderate. Eventually (years later) I figured out that she was always completely present in the moment. Her event-orientation is demonstrated through her focus on the person and the conversation she is having in the moment, and it's a wonderful quality. As spouses and friends, we continue to learn from each other and communicate through our different perspectives of time.

Often, time can feel like the one thing we *can't* offer others. But as it continues to remain necessary to the development of deepening relationships, we'll need to come up with creative solutions to our time poverty. If you, or the people in your life need some suggestions for working in more intentional communication, here are just a few tips:

## DEEP INSTEAD OF WIDE

I know it's exciting to have a plethora of "friends" online, and I certainly don't dismiss the ever-expanding opportunities social media offers us for connection, but we need to focus our time on the few friendships that have the potential to "go deep." In his life, Jesus focused on a handful of individuals with whom he would go deep, and the effects of those friendships rippled throughout history. Instead of trying to maintain 100 acquaintances, can we invest ourselves in three good friends? This will allow for greater transformation in the life of both the leader and follower.

## SHARED LIFE

We sometimes approach friendship as something that exists outside "real" life. We get this picture of it happening in a coffee shop, at an office meeting or through a weekend getaway. Instead, we can consider how to weave friendship into our daily living. Can we do our grocery shopping together? Can we go for a morning run together? If we're going to the same conference, can we carpool? This may be harder between cross-attraction friendships (a subject we examine more in chapter 10), but creative planning within groups of friends can still make this a possibility.

## PLANNING FOR FRIENDSHIP

I get it—we all want that effortless friendship, the illusive "organic" kind, the one we don't have to work at. But in the meantime, we would be wise to make conscientious and intentional space for friendship. Waiting for the day when you and your friend both happen to be free will be fruitless, and could communicate that you aren't willing to prioritize the friendship. So the next time you hear yourself uttering the phrase, "Let's get together sometime," whip out your phone or pocket calendar and pick a date.

## OPPORTUNITY COST

Every time we say yes to one thing, we say no to something else. Instead of saying yes to everything and everyone, can we do a better job measuring the opportunity cost of every commitment? Do you *have* to attend that one function? Must you take that phone call in the middle of dinner? Each choice, big or small, has a ripple effect, subtly shifting the opportunities available to us.

## GIVING MARGIN TO LIFE

I'll be the first one to admit my weakness in this area as I have been accused of leaving little margin in my schedule. I stack events on top of each other, generally keeping me running from one commitment to the next. If a friend should happen to need me, I have nothing to give them. (Can you tell I'm a time-oriented person?) So I started leaving fifteen minute buffers between appointments. This may not seem like a lot of time, but it's surprising what that little bit of margin can do.

## STAY AWARE

Your new friend could come from the most unlikely of places. When we move around our world in a flurry of activity, we could miss out on a friendship that is ready to develop. Stay aware of the unlikely but natural sources of friendship in life, and of the small—but meaningful—ways you can build those.

## QUALITY NOT QUANTITY

To truly have deep rooted relationships, it takes more than the accumulation of meaningless minutes—strong friendships require quality, life-giving experiences. It's not only important that we invest time, but that we invest it well. Consider each time investment in your friendships—is it of quality?

## RESPECT THE SEASON

As you invest time, give each other space to walk through certain seasons. Several factors could make us or our friends less available for an extended period of time: new babies, jobs that require a move, family tragedy, just to name a few. When the time truly isn't there, we need to be willing to extend some grace and space. If you're the one in that season and you just can't find any extra time for friends, communicate that with them upfront so they don't wonder why you've suddenly disappeared. If I'm describing a friend you currently have, let them off the hook. Let the time you've *already* invested in the relationship buoy you through this season to the next. Let them know you'll always be ready and willing to pour time into the friendship, but you respect the season they're in and can wait for them to be ready.

While I am sure there are many more ways to create the time and space for friendship, these are just a few from my experience. In Friendship Leadership, we need that time investment for trust to form, for intimacy to flourish, and for transformation to occur. In time, we reveal who we really are and can accept others as they really are—friend, follower and leader alike.

## Loyalty and Commitment

Have you ever been "ghosted"? Or perhaps you've done it yourself? Lately, there have been a number of articles written about the social phenomenon of "ghosting," both within the Christian community and the larger population. If you are unfamiliar with ghosting, it is defined as "practice of ending a personal relationship with someone by suddenly and without explanation withdrawing from all communication."[10] Variations of ghosting could include slowly (but deliberately) cutting someone out of a social group or personal relationship, usually in a process that leaves the abandoned party bewildered or uncomprehending.

---

10. www.dictionary.com.

In his blog post describing his personal experience with ghosting after presenting concerns to church leadership, Dr. Benjamin L. Corey (author of *Unafraid: Moving Beyond Fear-Based Faith*) shares:

> I made many "errors," and the net result was the tension in our little group continued to increase until my best friend bailed instead of navigating conflict—taking the rest of our social circle with him. We went from texting countless times a day and spending individual, and family time together, to . . . nothing.
>
> Quiet. Silence. Distance. Nonexistence.
>
> It was like a magician showed up in my life, covered everything with a blanket, and then with a whisk of the wand it all disappeared—leaving me just holding a blanket.
>
> The damage wasn't just something I suffered—I also had to navigate hard discussions with my then 12 year old daughter as to why she lost all her friends as well. I still wake up every morning and try to extend grace for the sin of ghosting, but the fact my daughter had her closest friends ghosted from her as well, is something I still struggle to forgive.[11]

Maybe you've been through something similar—maybe that's why you don't know if you trust the idea of friendship. This is painful enough on its own, but compounded with the sense of rejection and humiliation we can feel as leaders when this occurs within our churches, organizations, businesses or ministries.

But how about the other side? When we are the ones doing the ghosting? It is with shame that I look back on more immature times in my life when I found it easier to "fade someone out" of my inner circle, because I simply didn't want to deal with them. I know better now, a fact which allows me to reconcile some of those relationships.

There are certainly attractive elements to this method of resolving conflict (as opposed to healthier forms of conflict resolution). When a leader chooses to ghost someone else, they are removing not only the "problem," but also who they believe is the "problem person." In one sweeping motion, all issues (current and future) are removed. It saves a leader from having to go through the painful, awkward, potentially back-firing process

---

11. Corey, "Christian Ghosting."

of opening up, sharing feelings, and giving someone the opportunity to respond. But friendship requires the qualities of loyalty and commitment if trust is going to grow.

"But what about Matthew 18:17?," someone might ask. "Doesn't that give me the right to cut an offensive person out of my life?"

In that passage, Jesus describes a process of conflict resolution and the many steps one has to cover before even considering ending a relationship with an offender. First of all, we need to express our feelings to the person who hurt us. If that doesn't work, we bring a few more friends into the situation, peace-making friends who also embody the qualities of friendship this book has been describing. If that doesn't work, then we get leadership involved. If you are the leader in your context, to whom do you go for guidance? Call them up. And if all that doesn't work, for the sake of healthy boundaries, some relational distance may be required. But I want to point out why this process is not "ghosting," but actually a demonstration of loyalty and commitment:

1. Out of loyalty, the offended person approaches the offender in private. This gives the offender the benefit of the doubt, and respects their privacy.

2. The offender then is fully aware of the pain their actions have caused (as opposed to a ghosted person who is abandoned without explanation). Commitment to friendship compels the offended person to communicate fully with the offender, believing relationship with that person is worth the vulnerability required.

3. If things don't go well early on, the offended party does the opposite of isolate: they invite the participation of other who are wiser and more experienced.

4. In every step of the conflict resolution process, commitment to friendship and loyalty to a person guides each along a productive pathway toward reconciliation.

Commitment and loyalty include the quality of acceptance and create an environment of safety. Just because we voluntarily enter the process of friendship doesn't mean we aren't responsible for its continued health. When our friends know we're not going to suddenly disappear on them (as so many others do in our culture), when they can expect our continued presence in their lives, there will be space and trust for mutual transformation.

Additionally, this commitment and loyalty manifests itself outside of interpersonal conflict. Friendship requires continued presence even in the midst of chaos or crisis. A friend is willing to be present when difficult things happen, when life grows wearying or friends fall short. As Wuthnow describes it, "A solid commitment to relationships and to community takes time and sacrifice and the patience to endure failure."[12]

Loyalty and commitment are expressed through honesty, confidentiality and protection, especially when a crisis takes place. Can our friends count on us when the journey of life takes a turn off the sunny path and into the darkened woods of despair, discomfort or discouragement?

"It is fit for serene days, and graceful gifts, and country rambles, but also for rough roads and hard fare, shipwreck, poverty, and persecution."[13]

Loyal and committed friendship weathers it all.

How does this look in Friendship Leadership? Perhaps it means giving someone a little time and space to own their failures, grace to accept the humanity in them, privacy as they walk through challenging processes, and an enduring presence through it all. Friendship Leadership is also knowing when to ask for those things for ourselves. It's choosing not to gossip, choosing to speak life, choosing to hold on when others lose patience, choosing to pick up the phone, even when we know it won't be good news. It's staying committed in prayer, loyal to the image of God in our friends, relying on the divine example of presence and sacrifice instead of the human tendency to "ghost." Friends accept each other, mutually aware of the other's weaknesses, failures and mistakes. Transparency, authenticity, vulnerability and sinfulness are met with grace, love and loyalty.

## Priority

I remember sitting at the dinner table with my boss and a few other co-workers. We were out of town for our staff retreat, which was due to begin the next day. A handful of us had been able to escape the office a day early and we were now enjoying a quiet dinner. As we sat there, I couldn't help but feel a little guilty thinking of the other staff members who hadn't been able to come up early and would be joining us the next day. They were missing out on a lovely meal and good conversation. As the dinner drew to a close, our boss insisted on paying for the group, which only compounded

12. Wuthnow, *Sharing the Journey*, 17.
13. Stade, *Essays and Poems*, 180.

my guilt. Finally, I spoke up, admitting that I felt badly for accepting this gift of time, food, and friendship, when it couldn't be given to everyone on our staff. I remember my boss responding with sincerity, quoting an Andy Stanley book: "Do for one what you wish you could do for everyone."[14]

In that moment, I recognized that my own need for what I considered "fairness" could paralyze me from investing in friendships with coworkers, bosses, or subordinates. Often, when it comes to the intermingling of friendship and leadership, this can become a point of inaction. Our fear of inequality can become an excuse to do nothing. We don't add priority to our relationships simply *because* we cannot do it for everyone. But think about the implications of this way of thinking: I am a pastor of a church with a weekend attendance of about 1,000 people. I cannot become "best friends" with everyone in my congregation; neither can I prioritize each of those relationships equally. If I were to allow the fear of that inequality to dictate my relationships, I wouldn't have *any* friendships. This is one of the main reasons why pastors and leaders often find themselves isolated and lonely.

In the story above, my boss saw an opportunity to do for some staff members what he wished he could do for all. I also realized that, in the future, he would extend that same graciousness to the coworkers who were missing from dinner that night. It was a matter of investing the relationships he could, while he could. In friendship, we have the opportunity to live out the gracious acts we wish we could do for all. By showing a priority for friendship, my boss took advantage of an opportunity to infuse value into his relationships. As I look at my leadership, I add priority to the friendships I can, and encourage my friends and staff to do the same. I cannot befriend everyone to the level I have been describing in this chapter, but I can create and encourage an environment in which everyone is being a friend to, and receiving friendship from, someone else. I am capable of adopting the disposition of a friend in most relationships, even when my available time is less than I would like. The worst thing I could do, however, is avoid all friendships because I cannot offer the same type, or level, of friendship to everyone in my sphere of influence.

As I think about this idea of giving priority to the relationships and friendships God places in our path, I am reminded of the many healings of Jesus. Though he had the power to heal everyone in a town, or the nation, or even the entire world, he usually limited himself to healing the person

14. Stanley, *Deep and Wide*, 42.

right in front of him. He prioritized the people along his individual path, but commissioned his disciples to then go and heal those they encountered. As leaders, we are allowed to give priority to our friendships; through this implicit example and our explicit teachings, we can also encourage others to do the same, creating an environment in which friendship flourishes.

I have to make friendship a life priority in order to have relationships of depth. Friendships will be crowded out by administration, errands, interruptions, and deadlines, unless they are prioritized through intentional time investment. Sometimes, this prioritization is the result of careful planning; other times, it involves allowing our priorities to determine the actions of the next five minutes. It reflects the value that people are more important than programs, and relationships are more important than results. This value will impact the depth of the relationship and the subsequent influence that comes from that relationship. It's human nature that people have a tendency to like people who reward them, a fact proven through classical conditioning theory.[15] A relationship with generosity, encouragement, and preference will be the kind of relationship that is attractive and rewarding. Demonstrating preference creates a dynamic and attractive relationship.

In addition to giving contextual priority to friendships, we also need to make our friends "number one," preferring them above ourselves.[16] As love infuses friendship, we continue to view the friend as the priority—above our goals, our ambitions, our needs, and our desires. Loving leadership sets the tone of the relationships by first placing the friend above us, and priority reminds us to stay that way.

You may be tempted to ask with concern, "How do we demonstrate a priority for friendship, while avoiding favoritism?" A good question, as there exists the danger of favoritism that can come from working with friends, whether the favoritism is actual or perceived. There must be an awareness of this potential perception, as well as its real danger. In reference to workplace goals, objectivity must be maintained in spite of closer personal attachments to friends. Being as fair and equitable as possible in the treatment of all concerns and ideas is critical to avoiding this danger. Favoritism is what occurs when boundaries are neglected, when emotional intelligence is lacking, or when the timing of appropriate behavior is disregarded. I may show priority for a friendship by having that friend over for dinner; that doesn't mean the friend will automatically have the winning

15. Fehr, *Friendship Processes*, 40.

16. Engstrom and Larson, *The Fine Art of Friendship*, 101.

vote in a workplace disagreement. Priority is demonstrated in discretionary times. Favoritism is an unhealthy and immature deviation from priority.

With healthy and communicated boundaries, friendship is the expression of giving those along our path priority in our lives. We recognize them and do for them what we wish we could do for everyone. We boldly invest in relationships, with wisdom, discretion and joy.

## Communication

When friends reunite, communication flows. We catch up on life. We have stories to tell. We fill the time with talk. In every description of friendship I've read, communication is listed as a key skill. Friends are involved in mutual sharing and listening as they live life together. In his book, *Friendship*, Jim Conway lists six different "skills for deep and lasting friendships;" four of those six skills focus on the actions required in communication: attending, listening, talking and affirmation.[17] It seems like one of the more obvious traits of friendship (don't we all generally love talking with our friends?); yet taking this skill for granted can lead to an underdeveloped set of communication skills. Just because we like to talk for hours, doesn't necessarily mean we're good at communication. If anything, with friends and family alike, true communication can fall to the wayside as we overlook the finer points of communication.

Communication is not just talking, but learning how to engage in empathetic listening. Listening is perhaps the most important part of communication. Consequently, improving listening skills enhances one's ability to be a good friend. Perhaps you've had this happen: you're sitting with a friend and you realize it's been forty-five minutes since you've been able to add anything to the conversation. You end up walking away from the encounter a little emptier than when you started. If you're like me, you may have even nodded off somewhere in the middle of their monologue. Or perhaps you've been the one to do more than your fair share of talking: you see their eyes glaze over, they start to fidget in their chair, and it dawns on you that you've been reciting a monologue that would make Shakespeare proud.

Of course, there are times in life, special circumstances which would require one friend to do the majority of the talking and the other to do the majority of the listening (as in times of crisis, tragedy, or loss). But if you

---

17. Conway, *Friendship*, 152.

start to notice a pattern of this one-sided communication, you might not be in a friendship—one of you might be treating the other as a personal counselor. Try to invest yourself as a proactive listener, asking questions and responding with genuine empathy.

While some may struggle with the listening component of communication, others may have a hard time sharing. For those who find expressions of vulnerability challenging, they may choose to hide behind the role of "listener" to keep from ever having to share real feelings and ideas. Sometimes this crosses the line into what I call "communicative martyrdom;" it's the person who takes pride in their ability to "be a good listener," deriving a sense of worth from their inability to talk about themselves. This is usually brought on by a belief that their feelings and ideas aren't worth the attention of others, or a low self-esteem that is bolstered by the compliments of others ("Wow! I've been talking for hours! You're such a great listener!") Leaders especially can be guilty of this; we hide our vulnerabilities and true selves as an "act of service." In every friendship, as trust and intimacy are established, communication will need to take on a form that represents the health and nature of the relationship. Listening and sharing must both be present for depth and longevity to exist.

This type of communication usually can't be achieved over an afternoon—a great deal of time is required for the development of healthy communication. In *Reclaiming Friendship*, Fernando paints this picture: "One of the keys to deep friendships is time spent in long conversations."[18] In a fast-paced world, time investment can be one of the hardest aspects of communication. Between work, school, community and home commitments, it seems like very little time is left for those "long conversations." We have just enough time to shoot out a three-word text message before we're flying off to the next event. But this way of communication takes its toll: "Most people today would say that they don't have time for this type of extended contact with people. So friendship has become something cheap and shallow."[19] Communication takes time, and friendships suffer when time is not invested in the friendship. Communication is a skill that only improves with time and deliberate effort.

Like most skills, if you're not good at communication, you can actually learn how to do it better. Some people have that natural ability to draw others in, to create the impression of friendship and security. My wife is

18. Fernando, *Reclaiming Friendship*, 140.
19. Fernando, *Reclaiming Friendship*, 12.

this kind of person. She gives people her undivided attention. Time stops, and she is absorbed in the moment of the conversation with her friends (whereas I usually am worried about the next thing I need to do). Honestly, I envy those people. I have to work at my communication—from my body language and vocal fluctuations to my focused listening and the practice of slowing down. Each of these forms the foundation of my communication with my friends, and each was a skill learned. A growing social awareness and emotional intelligence can bring much success to your communication endeavors within your friendships. And even if you think you're good at it, there's always room to improve.

One of my responsibilities as a pastor is leading couples through marriage counseling. There is a whole section devoted to communication and learning how a partner may hear or understand different messages. We deliberately work on inviting each person into the process of sharing and listening, repeating back what's been communicated to sharpen the skill of communication in each person. This same process of honing the communicative process can be revitalizing to any friendship. Communication is a necessity that facilitates healthy friendship where two souls are able to come together as one.

In the scope of Friendship Leadership, communication can be risky business. We worry that if we listen, will they take advantage of us? If we share, will they use that information against us? Will it impede my ability to lead? Scary as it may be, we need to take that risk and push ourselves toward better communication. Friendship and leadership both require this skill. When a leadership role and a friendship are both being maintained, the need for clear communication is accentuated. This allows for the creation and expression of understanding, respect, boundaries, and fair treatment in the workplace.

Communication is a tool that gives us a voice in our friendships with those we lead or follow. It enables us to have hard conversations with truth and grace, weaving personal understanding and empathy into the narrative of the relationship. It is the means by which we will know and be known. It is the sharing of souls along the journey.

## Encouragement

Lasting friends are those who have developed a strong sense of affirmation in a relationship, who can discern the gracious and hopeful truth of God and communicate it through life-giving words. They are fun to be around and leave people feeling better about themselves. Friends often believe in each other more than a person believes in him or herself, and have the capacity of speaking that reality into existence. As we name the positive qualities in our friends, they begin to believe in it, too.

Does this mean all friendships are supposed to be a festival of flattery? Hardly. I suppose you've probably witnessed this scenario before: two individuals gushing fake praise in an attempt to gain influence or reputation. From the outside, it's mildly nauseating. But what's the difference? How can we be encouragers without devolving into flatterers?

There are two primary differences between those two postures: truth and motivation. As Christian leaders, we have the ability to tap into the greater truth, through the Bible and the Holy Spirit. We are not limited to speaking to the surface ("What a great haircut!"), but can affirm the deeper aspects of the individual ("I'm proud of you for forgiving your step-father. I know that was hard.") Not that the first example is wrong, but which of the two has a greater chance of actually encouraging the journey of the friend? Honest affirmation in friendship can heal and transform.

Additionally, spiritual affirmation speaks the truth, even if it's hard to hear at times. Flattery won't do that. But we have a way of encouraging one another to do and be their best. We can help people reach their maximum potential and challenge them to keep growing. In other words, we are able to confront, challenge, and help our friends to see themselves as they really are. We continue to extend acceptance while challenging our friends to not remain the same. We accept who they are, not trying to change them ourselves but spurring on the life-changing work of God in them. We see both the current and eternal realities of who they are, walking alongside our friends as those two realities unify within them. I have been deeply impacted by friends who have seen me for who I could be. They had a higher view of me than I had of myself (and they were right about me). This has helped me overcome my negative self-talk. Encouragement can and should be prophetic.

In challenging our motivations, we can root out flattery by discovering our own selfish ambitions. This is a bit harder to discern at times, both within ourselves and within others. There may even be a mixed bag of motivations that we need to sort through. Let me give you an example of when I have to really exercise this discernment in my own life. Every year, there is a national conference for my denomination. Leaders from around the world gather for four days in one city. Some leaders are highly influential in the denomination, and others have only begun to develop a reputation. As I wander through those crowds, deciding with whom I should spend time and what I should say, I try to bring my words and actions into alignment with life-giving truth. Am I complimenting the ministry of a well-known pastor because I want them to like me? Because perhaps I can use them as a catalyst for my own ministry? Do I speak life and affirmation into the small-church pastor's life, as I would the mega-church's pastor? My own motivation reveals the difference between true encouragement and mere flattery.

Having rooted out flattery, we can lean into the encouragement and affirmation we want to give to and receive from friends. We can probably all recall times when we felt vulnerable receiving feedback. Leaders generally have to sift through a volley of both solicited and unsolicited flattery and criticism, not knowing which feedback to trust and internalize, and what to dismiss. A friend who can give the honest truth is invaluable. And if you are friends with your leader, look for ways to speak positive truth (not flattery)—they need it. As trust is developed, don't disregard your ability to speak some of the "spurring on" words in gentle love. Oftentimes, what a leader needs most is a friend who will be honest, loving, gentle and kind. This doesn't make you a "fan," it makes you a friend, especially if your feedback is life-giving and truthful.

If you are friends with the people following you, remember that their accomplishments in life are just as important as yours. The person speaking to crowds of thousands is no more worthy of encouragement than the schoolteacher speaking to a class of twenty five-year-olds. Yet sometimes, the follower can feel overshadowed by the leader, sensing that their experiences and feelings are not as valid. This can generate a bitterness within the friendship and sour it to the point of ruin. The reality is that each of you is living out the calling of God, each of you has trials to overcome, and both of you deserve recognition and support. If, as a leader, you enter a friendship hoping for fans, you will be disappointed with a string of short-lived relationships. Instead, cultivate a friendship with a mind motivated to encourage and affirm—with your time, attention, words and actions. Your friends are worthy of it.

Ephesians 4:29 says that the words we speak should "be helpful for building each other up according to their needs, that it may benefit those who listen." Building communication skills, as we mentioned earlier, can assist any attempts at encouragement, making sure that we truly are offering words that take into consideration the needs of our friend, and are received as beneficial. As someone who is friends with my leaders, and friends with those whom I lead, I can speak to the truth of this statement: one of the greatest gifts we can offer our friends is life-giving words that speak the truth as God reveals it.

## Respect

In our family, we called the three bedrooms downstairs in our home "The Girl's Dorm." Three single women, all in their 20s, shared the space. While some paid rent, others would babysit our two small children on occasion as part of their "rental agreement." As you can imagine, this was a great blessing to my wife and me. We were able to enjoy dates nights every week. This arrangement worked for the mutual benefit of everybody involved.

Over the years, we have had many singles live with us. Exchange students. Interns. Staff members. Men and women. We have opened up our home in this way to exercise Friendship Leadership. While we recognize the caution that must be exercised in relationships of intimacy because of our over sexualized culture (a topic we'll revisit in chapter 10), for now, I want to mention that respect is an essential ingredient in all friendships and it combats the temptations that come with sexual brokenness—a reality for so many people. 1 Timothy 5:1–2 commands us to "Treat younger men as brothers, older women as mothers and younger women as sisters, with absolute purity." As a quality of Friendship Leadership, respect is a safeguard against all kinds of abuse.

It should go without saying that friends respect each other. The story above is just one example of the many reasons why respect must inhabit the foundation of any friendship, as an expression of the love in the relationship. Even if we do not agree with the actions or choices of our friend, we still respect them as a person. When respect is lost, the quality of friendship is lost.

How can we be sure respect is present in the relationship? Well, first it needs to be centered in the identity of who each person is: made in the image of God. This idea of *Imago Dei* informs the way we perceive and approach one another. In addition to that theological principle, we find other biblical examples of this idea of finding God in humanity. In the famous parable of the "Sheep and the Goats" (Matt 25:31–46), Jesus reminds us that whatever we do to each other, we are doing to him. Hebrews 13 exhorts us to welcome strangers, for in so doing, we could be "entertaining angels," again illustrating the respect intrinsically found within each person as a creation loved by God. I also respect people because God values them—Ephesians 2:10 describes them as "God's handiwork," an expression of his creativity and love, purchased by his blood. We are called to see the God-value placed in each person, looking up to others instead of down on them. Finally, Philippians 2:3 encourages us to "do nothing out of selfish ambition or vain conceit. Rather, in humility value others" above ourselves. We are called to a posture of looking up to others, instead of looking down on them.

Respect in the realm of leadership is often presented, if not consciously, then unconsciously, as a one-sided affair, where the follower respects the leader. This is usually based upon a title (earned or bestowed), a rank, a reputation, or certain achievements. Within my personal sphere of influence, I know of several "leaders" who spend more time preoccupied with the respect they feel they are due (or are being denied) than they are building up and respecting others. One of my least favorite demands of some leaders is to respect the office. ("I am the Lord's anointed, and you cannot raise your hand against the Lord's anointed," or "It's not about me, it's about the office that I hold.") To me, this is a twisting of Scripture to create fear and power over others. It is mutual respect that makes friendship between leaders and subordinates possible. Yes, a leader should be respected (the exact nature and expression of this respect is dependent on the culture), but I would suggest a true leader *leads* others into relationships of respect by first demonstrating it. Want to be more respected in your position/ministry/business/corporation? How much are you respecting others?

This can be a painfully patient process, depending on the health and past experiences of those in the friendship. If a leader hasn't healed from past rejection or betrayal, those wounds could lead to an unproductive emphasis on the respect due him/her. If someone following a leader has experienced spiritual abuse or manipulation in the past, or feels a general lack of concern or respect for them as a person, they will most likely deny respect to their current leader, even within a friendship. It takes someone with a gentle and humble heart (usually someone who has healed and grown from their own past pain) to break the unhealthy cycle of demanding, rather than offering, respect.

I was speaking with a choir director recently who shared about her experience trying to lead a group of twenty to thirty musicians, of varying age and experience, through a musical season:

> Every once and a while, a person would complain loudly if they weren't understanding how to read the sheet music or if they couldn't hear their part. Other times, they would develop a negative attitude about someone else in the choir—they didn't like how they sang (too loud, too quiet, too stylized, too showy, too diva, etc.), how they stood, or how they approached the music-learning process. Most of the time, this frustration would be vented at me, the leader of the group. It would generally be expressed in a disrespectful comment or tone.
>
> In that moment, as the whole choir watched me, I knew I had a choice in how I was going to respond. I knew I was well within my rights to snap back, to remind them that I was the "Choir Director," and that they were lucky to be there in the first place. I could even ask them to leave. But instead, I would extend empathy, listen to the concern underlying the disrespect, and speak directly to the frustrated individual. I would choose to offer respect and patience. The complainer would immediately respond to my respectful posture: all their anger would deflate, they would offer an apology, and then change their attitude. They would respect me more going forward, as would the rest of the choir, because I respected them. Respect leads to respect—very rarely does it not work out.[20]

Within a friendship, respect is vital for the relationship to work. It fluctuates throughout seasons of leadership, taking on new dynamics with each new set of circumstances. If respect is lost because of the friendship, then the work relationship is compromised and becomes unhealthy.

In order to safeguard healthy respect in Friendship Leadership, both people should consider the elements of space and boundaries. In giving space, friends don't overwhelm each other with their demands. Both the one who leads and the one who follows must be careful to avoid becoming possessive. Possessiveness will put a strain on any friendship. A leader who doesn't want to share their friends with others, or demands too much in terms of time, dependence (leading to codependency), or commitment

20. Rachel McMurray-Branscombe, in discussion with Matt Messner, July 2017.

can end up being a negative force in the life of a friend. The leader friend can suffer a feeling of personal rejection if they are unwilling to offer space to their friends. If the friend who follows becomes possessive, they could attempt manipulation in order to control the leader friend. They could also have their feelings hurt often if they don't understand the nature of giving space to their leader friend. A healthy balance must be achieved, including shared experience, intimacy, and time together, without being codependent.

For this reason, I have found that establishing clear boundaries is necessary for a respectful relationship. When friends work for each other, or with each other, boundaries must be clear, distinguishing between how one relates in or outside the work environment. This has to do with what is talked about, how the time is spent, and how communication takes place with each other. Generally, work objectives must not be set aside to nurture friendship while on the job. The nurturing aspect of friendship is best kept outside the work environment. This avoids some of the pitfalls of having "dual relationships," and maintains a higher degree of professionalism. Likewise, when I am outside the "work environment," I often prefer to focus on developing the personal side of the friendship. My friends who have been under my leadership know that when I'm at home, I would much prefer to talk about good books or music than anything happening in the "office." For me, this keeps the relationship well-rounded and healthy. You may have to experiment with what works for you. But I can tell you this much: a friendship without any boundaries will quickly grow unhealthy.

When it comes to respect in Friendship Leadership, I encourage you to take the first step. Freely offer your respect to others, if for no other reason than in respect for the image of God dwelling in them. Respect your friends as you would hope to be respected. Give space and receive it warmly. Experiment with and communicate your boundaries; ask your friends what theirs might be. In this way, you can set your friendship up for success.

## Intimacy

Perhaps one of the most feared and simultaneously craved qualities of friendship is intimacy. While we all want to be known, we can also fear the vulnerability that comes with deepening intimacy. Without it, however, friendships will barely scratch the surface of true identity, making transformation impossible.

In basic terms, intimacy is the sharing of one's life and self. Intimacy is achieved through communication and mutual disclosure, and requires an intentional effort. It involves a choice to be vulnerable. Intimacy is one of the goals of marriage (becoming "one" in every way), and involves a complete sharing of the total self, for life. Intimacy goes deeper than superficial conversations about weather. It includes the multiple dimensions of life: emotions, spiritual struggles, hopes, dreams, and more. Aristotle describes the intimacy of friendship as one soul abiding in two bodies.[1] Friendship engages people for who they are, not merely what they do. Intimacy negates using friendship to accomplish one's own goals, as it requires mutuality and respect. It sees beyond a persons' creativity, talent, possessions, or usefulness. Through intimacy, friendship goes beyond the peripherals of life.

In his book about building friendships, best-selling author Alan Loy McGinnis encourages relationships to "cultivate transparency."[2] While I mentioned "disclosure" in the definition of friendship, I also believe it's a skill that requires constant growth and investment. Transparency and self-disclosure are closely related elements that characterize the intimacy found in friendships. "As a relationship progresses, the breadth and depth of self-disclosure increases."[3] This factor distinguishes acquaintances from friends. Friendships progress as personal information is exchanged. As this is done reciprocally, intimacy increases, and friendship grows. As Jesus spent time with the disciples, their relationship moved to deeper levels. As he revealed more about himself to them, the relationship grew beyond one of strictly being their rabbi or master, to a relationship of intimacy characterized as friendship.

In order to create the right environment for transparency, friends exercise mutual trust. Trust creates a feeling of safety and confidence that one will neither be betrayed nor hurt by a friend. Truth, honesty, and loyalty all lead to a deepening sense of trust in a friendship. This leads also to a greater openness, honesty, sincerity and disclosure. Regarding the essential element of trust, the philosopher Cicero poignantly states, "Now the foundation of that steadfastness and loyalty for which we are looking in friendship is trust, for nothing endures that cannot be trusted."[4]

---

1. Black, *The Art of Being a Good Friend*, 12.
2. McGinnis, *The Friendship Factor*, 22.
3. McGinnis, *The Friendship Factor*, 178.
4. Pakaluk, *Other Selves*, 103.

This value of trust is especially critical in Friendship Leadership. A leader needs to know they can reveal their true self, receiving acceptance and privacy in return. A follower needs to feel they can reveal their true self, knowing the information won't be used as fodder for judgment or manipulation. Trust includes believing the best in the other, in their words and actions. It means giving our friends the benefit of the doubt, resisting the urge to shut everyone out. This can be especially challenging if we've been hurt in the past.

But isn't it true that we can be hurt by all this vulnerability and intimacy? Yes. I wish I could offer you a pain-free guarantee, but that is beyond me. It happened to Jesus and it will happen to us. It is a risk we take, believing that we are not called to close ourselves off out of fear. Jesus is equipped to walk us through the pain when it occurs. Personally, I allowed this fear to dictate the levels of intimacy in my friendships for some time, until I read this quote by C.S. Lewis, found in his description of *agapé* love:

> To love at all is to be vulnerable. Love anything and your heart will be wrung and possibly broken. If you want to make sure of keeping it intact you must give it to no one, not even an animal. Wrap it carefully round with hobbies and little luxuries; avoid all entanglements. Lock it up safe in the casket or coffin of your selfishness. But in that casket, safe, dark, motionless, airless, it will change. It will not be broken; it will become unbreakable, impenetrable, irredeemable. To love is to be vulnerable.[5]

Surrendering to vulnerability calls us onto a path of faith, and it is that very faith that imbues the friendship with deep, rich intimacy. It is only when we've risked, and, holding our breath, stood in that moment between reward and despair at the hand of our friend, that we can appreciate the depth of trust in the relationship. When we reveal the dark doubt, the struggle, the pain, the hope, and still receive acceptance, grace and love, we can begin to understand the nature of our friendship with God, the divine friendship inspiring us on earth.

---

5. Lewis, *The Four Loves*, 111.

# 6

## People in Friendship Leadership

ON THE SURFACE, IT can seem easy to discuss Friendship Leadership from a purely theoretical perspective. But friendship involves people—real, living, breathing people. People who find themselves in complicated circumstances, who walk the lines of maturity and appropriate behavior, who strive for love because of, and in spite of, their humanity. These are the people who make Friendship Leadership possible: you and I. Within our relationships, we occupy different roles, we take on different types of relationships. A diverse life will lead to a variety of most of these types and role sets of friendship. Knowing who you are—and who others can possibly be—in your relationships will empower all your efforts in Friendship Leadership.

This chapter will examine each of the types of friendship we experience: friendship with God, with self, and with others. Each of these types of friendship builds upon the previous, creating a solid foundation for life-long and fulfilling relationships. The final section of the chapter will identify the three different role sets in our workplace relationships. As we hope to utilize friendship as an expression of leadership in a broader environment, we first need to examine how the context will influence us.

As people following the way of Friendship Leadership, let's look at these different types of friendship:

### Friendship with God

Growing up in a rural community on the Oregon Coast, our property had no fences. I was surrounded by endless wilderness, an estuary teeming with life, and a few other kids who spent their hours building forts, riding BMX, shooting BB guns, and playing every game under the sun. The environment itself awakened an awe for the creation and a wanderlust to explore.

My family wasn't religious at all. We did church in our living room. My mom played the piano and we read stories from a children's Bible purchased at the county fair. Belief was assumed and very real for me. I had a small Gideon's Bible that I treasured as much as any of my possessions. One day I could not find it. I obsessively looked for it for years.

At the age of ten, I read a story about a child who had a friendship with God. This concept caused my heart to leap and to dream. Could I be that child? Was it possible to have a friendship with the Creator? From that unforgettable moment until now, I have been in a friendship with God. At times, it has been rocky as I haven't always been a good friend. I left my Friend for a dark season. I didn't always invest in the friendship. I denied my Friend. Yet he has been faithful, steadfast, gracious, and relentlessly tenacious in his pursuit of me. The Divine Friendship provides a foundation for all human friendship. The hymn writer, Jospeh Scriven, said it well: "What a friend we have in Jesus."

Friendship and faith go hand-in-hand. On the one hand, as Weatherhead notes in *The Transforming Friendship*, "Christianity is the acceptance of the gift of the friendship of Jesus."[1] On the other hand, friendship cannot grow to its full potential without the love, acceptance, and forgiveness we experience through God's presence in our lives. With this in mind, before we can consider other forms of types of friendship, we begin with the most foundational friendship in existence: our friendship with our Creator.

In the process of growing in a strong friendship with God, Christians will also grow to appreciate who they are—they are beloved by God as one of his unique children. Friendship with God is the highest form of friendship one can have. An ability to accept oneself as God's friend increases a person's capacity to love others. We can give what we've received from God to those around us, and to ourselves. In Luke 7:47, Jesus declared that the person who has been forgiven much, loves much. The extent to which he offers us love, forgiveness and friendship fuels our own attempts at friendship. Thomas Aquinas wrote, "We may speak of charity in respect of its specific nature, namely as denoting man's friendship with God in the first place, and, consequently, with the things of God, among which things is

---

1. Weatherhead, *The Transforming Friendship*, 25.

man himself who has charity."[2] The cyclical nature of friendship with God and with people is a distinctive mark of Christian friendship.

This foundational friendship with God reflects a progression that takes place in spiritual growth: when a person comes to understand God's love, they come to understand their value, and then are able to love others as God's children. Our friendships with others and ourselves is an expression of our friendship with God. As David received friendship from God, so was he able to offer it to Jonathan. As Peter experience friendship with Jesus, so was he able to be a leader in the church.

At the same time, our friendship with others can be viewed by Christians as communion with God through another person—it's the coming together that undergirds all relationships in the universe. In Matthew 25:40, Jesus said we must see Christ in one another, even strangers: "Whatsoever you do to the least of my brothers, that you do unto me."

An intimate friendship offers more than a way to satisfy a basic human need for belonging; it offers a way to learn more about God's love for us through the love of another. We point each other in the direction of friendship, revealing a limited impression of the Great Friendship that is offered to us. Keaton writes, "Friends who share with us the love of God and act as our companions on the journey also direct us to deeper communion with Christ."[3]

This is the cycle of friendship: we can only begin to offer true friendship to others when we have received and understood it first from God; yet in our friendships with others, we are able to point each other back to the beloved first friendship, reflecting the source of the light of love.

These aspects of friendship are unique to the Christian experience. Aelred of Rievaulx, in *Spiritual Friendship*, argued that "true friendship cannot exist among those who live without Christ."[4] Although he acknowledges the existence of friendships outside of faith, he upholds the idea that true friendship has a divine element of love and the presence of Christ that requires faith. This distinction makes Christian friendship richer and deeper in its values and motives than the friendship outside the example and experience of God's friendship. The Good News makes friendship with God possible for the Christian because the Gospel is about God coming near and opening the way of deep communication, communion and fellowship

2. Pakaluk, *Other Selves*, 179.

3. Keaton, Friendship as Communion With God, 28.

4. Pakaluk, *Other Selves*, 134.

with him. We disregard this foundation of friendship to the detriment of all other relationships in our lives. Without the gift of God's friendship, our needs can consume our friendships, crippling them of their power to transform. Let us apply the qualities of friendship to God, giving and receiving: initiative, time, loyalty and commitment, priority, communication, encouragement, respect and intimacy.

## Friendship with Self

I was not a good friend to myself. I didn't like my skinniness. I despised my shyness. I was scathingly critical of my own failures—whether it was my inability to hit a baseball or my failure to get a good grade. Consequently, I worked obsessively to make a more likable me. One who was always loved by his parents (never disappointing or failing them).

Academics and athletics became the mediums I used to try to develop a self that I and others would love. I was taught to believe that these were the key ingredients to success, and success would bring happiness. If I achieved success in these things, I would be a good friend to myself. I would like myself if I was smarter, faster, more popular, better.

During high school, I ran seventy miles every week. Before and after school, I was logging miles pursuing the dream of success. Running was a great escape from my insecurities and I was good at it. Yet after winning the Cross Country State Championship, I stood on top of a platform with steps that only led one direction: down. The following season I would finish third with devastating disappointment. Although my grades were excellent, I did not become the valedictorian or the salutatorian, I graduated third in my class and there is no honorary title for that distinction.

The problem was that I would never measure up. I couldn't be the smartest. I couldn't be the fastest. I wasn't voted as the most popular in my class. I fell short and I didn't like this about myself. I was moving further and further away from friendship with self.

This may be God's biggest challenge in my life: teaching me to love myself. Not in a narcissistic, vainglorious way, but in a way that brings about congruency, peace, self-satisfaction, confidence, and security.

My Creator Friend is helping me with this essential part of my life as a disciple: I cannot love others well until I am able to truly love myself.

Let me describe a certain kind of person to you:

There is a person who desperately longs to have friends. They sense a deep emptiness at their core, yearning for authentic relationships (even just one) to fill their lack. They feel their impoverishment of friendship every day, in the silence of their home, in the empty chair next to them as they eat lunch, in the few invitations that come their way. They approach others with kind intention, and though that kindness is often returned, it is never transmuted into a real and lasting connection. This person is left feeling powerless and confused—*Why can everyone else make friends except for me?*

This isn't the whole story, however. Because what I haven't mentioned yet is this: the person hates themselves. Not in a loud, tangible way. In a quiet, more menacing way. In the way they draw away from others because they don't believe anyone else will want to hear what they have to say. In the way they put themselves down before anyone else has a chance to. In the way they don't invite anyone over because they don't have good food to share, funny stories to tell, or really, anything to offer. You can see it hiding behind the desperate smile: the plea for acceptance and approval. You get the sense they are starving themselves like social anorexics, needing the warmth and comfort of friendship, but sabotaging all their own efforts because of a deep (and perhaps unknown even to them) self-loathing.

Do you know this person? I do. I've known a few, in fact. And the hardest part is that while I can offer them my friendship, it cannot substitute for their own lack of friendship with themselves.

Friendship with oneself is a prerequisite to healthy friendship with others. The biblical mandate found in Matthew 19:19 is to "love your neighbor as yourself." A person must find peace with themselves, otherwise they will use and manipulate friendships to satisfy their own broken needs, and will not be able to enter into a friendship of mutuality. Emerson warns us, "We must be our own friend before we can be another's."[5]

If friendship is a goal we hope to achieve, we cannot cut the corner of friendship with self.

While there is too much to be said about depression, internal aggression, and self-loathing to cover it with any degree of comprehensiveness in this book, these maladies will certainly affect our friendship and leadership, and cannot therefore be disregarded. If these descriptors sound like you, I would recommend considering a visit to a counselor. The concept

5. Stade, *Essays and Poems*, 182.

of "loving others as we love ourselves" will be completely lost on one who cannot love themselves.

To address one concern, however, I want to focus on the question: where is the line between friendship with self, and a narcissistic self-love? A person consumed with self-love will habitually and greedily spend their time and resources on things that will indulge pleasure to themselves.[6] A healthy love for self comes from recognizing God's love and our value before him. The *character* of the person is the determining factor in how one's self-worth is either a benefit or a detriment to the development of friendship and care for others. A person who is at peace with themselves will be better able to care for and contribute to the needs of others because they feel good about themselves, whereas a needy person will never be satisfied with what the friendship offers them, and will be expressing an unquenchable desire for more than the relationship can offer.

Our friendship with self is built upon our friendship with God, and the faith we place in his truth. With these two friendships in place, we can offer up our friendship to others with a whole heart and healthy perspective.

## Friendship with Others

Moving to a new community was devastating to me. After nearly fifteen years at the same church, in the same city, my wife and I had moved from a suburb of Seattle to a small coastal community in Northern California. Our children opted to stay in Seattle and we had made the move with a deep sense of calling.

Immediately, I had to face the reality that I had no "real friends" in our new community. The ones I had left behind were rich and deep—filled with memories covering the full spectrum of life together. I understood that these friendships had taken fifteen years to develop in order to become what they were.

I knew I could and would keep some of my "old friends" through the virtual closeness available through technology and periodic visits. But Friendship Leadership demanded more of me in my new city.

Just a couple of months after the big move, I was having dinner with a church leader in my new home when his son spoke up, "You guys are best friends now, aren't you?"

6. Pakaluk, *Other Selves*, 62.

I liked the guy and I could tell we would become friends, but I defensively said, "Not really. We're just getting to know each other."

I felt guarded, still grieving friends left behind. I was tentatively putting my toes into the deep waters of new friendships.

I faced the decision of friendship in a new context: Would I give myself fully to the hard work necessary to start over again with new friends?

Perhaps it's a new season in life, a new school, a new job, or a new city—whatever the context, the thought of beginning anew can leave some shaken and anxious. There are those people who seem to possess the natural ability to win friends more easily. It is a strength of their personality, like others possess the ability to speak several languages, play an instrument, or run for miles more easily than others. They are often outgoing and gregarious in personality, drawing people to them, like moths to an effervescent flame.

But there are others who would identify as having a quiet, shy personality, and who may have great difficulty making friends. While it may not come as naturally to them, if the value of friendship, or the longing for relationship, is strong enough, shy people can overcome their fears, gaining skills and experience to strengthen their social abilities. They can move beyond halting passivity and become a person who isn't controlled by a fear of rejection. Yager warns of the effects of fear-based living in the workplace: "In most careers, it will stop you from advancing as far and as fast as you could and even how much daily enjoyment you get out of your work because your shyness stops you . . . Fortunately, there is help for those who are shy, from individual or group counseling to support groups as well as self-help books on overcoming shyness."[7]

Before moving forward, however, I do want to acknowledge the difference between a social shyness and a condition of anxiety. Some do suffer from debilitating social anxiety, and I do not wish to belittle their condition. If fear is debilitating and limiting to a person, they would do well to seek out the professional help that is available. In this section, I am focusing on the person for whom building friendships doesn't come as naturally as it does to others.

All this applies to making new friendships; but what about old friendships with others? The ones that fit us like worn, familiar clothes? They may be comfortable, but if we don't take care of these relationships, they can grow to be threadbare and tattered. For some readers, the call of this book

7. Yager, *Who's That Sitting At My Desk?*, 210.

isn't to develop new friendships, but rather to reinvest in the friendships you already have. As we build on the foundation of a friendship with God, who never forgets us, and a friendship with self, in which grace is daily extended, our friendships with others can demonstrate this same process of continual renewal. The time we have to invest in each other is so brief and limited, that good stewardship would remind us to appreciate and invest in our friendships with others.

## Role Sets within Friendship Leadership

I remember the first time I was placed in formal leadership over a group of my friends. I was nineteen and asked to be the coach of a group of interns, many of whom were my close friends. Some were older than me; others had been in the ministry program longer than I had. Some thought I was too young for the position, and still others wondered why they hadn't been chosen. To say the least, there was an uncomfortable shift in some of my relationships with my friends, and we each had to work at reestablishing the boundaries and characteristics of our friendships. I had to determine what it looked like to be friends with those under my leadership, and they had to decide if and how they were going to remain my friend given the new power dynamics in our ministry context.

I wish I could say that we handled it all gracefully, but as we were young and inexperienced, that wasn't necessarily the case. In the years since then, I've found it's helpful to understand the broader systemic dynamics in order to fully embody the roles within friendship. And make no mistake, both follower and friend have a role in the health and success of the friendship.

**Figure 1**

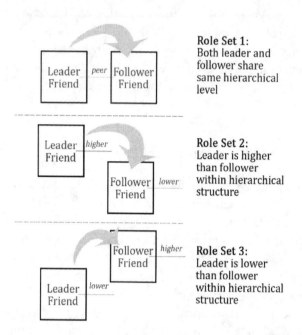

Role Set 1:
Both leader and
follower share
same hierarchical
level

Role Set 2:
Leader is higher
than follower
within hierarchical
structure

Role Set 3:
Leader is lower
than follower
within hierarchical
structure

As this book focuses on those friendships where leadership is an active presence, it follows that the friendship takes place within a larger organizational context. Maybe it's a formal structure (e.g. a corporate office), or a loose association (e.g. a community gathering). The organizational structure could be vertical in nature, with highly stratified levels of authority, or it could be horizontal, with decision-making and power equally distributed.

Within every context, there are three different role sets within which we and our friends could be classified. These correspond with Figure 1. In each set, there are three dynamics at work: the movement of natural leadership, the hierarchical placement, and friendship. Assuming we now see the benefits and need to incorporate friendship in our leadership, we now turn our attention to the roles which friend-leaders and friend-followers take. Before we look at these role sets, however, let's pause for a minute to talk about leadership. Remember that within the context of this book, leadership is not the "official" utilization of titles or positional leadership. Instead, leadership is referring to the influence of one person on another towards a greater love of God and people. In this way, leadership can occur irrespective of job title. One other important element of leadership is that it can be fluid within a relationship—one friend might lead for a while, and then follow, as the relationship builds over time. These are not meant to be understood as concrete roles, but rather living, growing, and evolving roles.

## Role Set 1: Friends Leading Peers

In this role set, two friends are on the same hierarchical level within the organizational structure. Neither has formal authority over the other, though one friend leads the other through their natural or learned leadership skills and influence. This is perhaps the most fluid as the barrier of hierarchical status is nonexistent—leadership can naturally flow from one friend to the other, and back again, as the situation warrants it. Also, this role set is most conducive for friendship development.

As a senior pastor, I have other senior pastor friends with whom I share a deep friendship. More than that, I am able to lead them through their dark moments, and they lead me through mine. We refine each other, and I find intimacy and trust to be most easily bestowed in this role set. As neither friend has official authority over the other, it lessens fears of abuse of power or manipulation. In this role set, friendship and leadership naturally walk hand-in-hand.

**Figure 2**

|  | Strengths | Weaknesses |
|---|---|---|
| *Role Set 1* | Easier to trust and develop intimacy | Vulnerable to jealousy, envy, unhealthy competition |
| *Role Set 2* | Clearly defined roles; naturally aligns with organizational structure | Vulnerable to fears of manipulation and power abuse (follower); fears of betrayal and rejection (leader) |
| *Role Set 3* | Humble truth-telling; broad respect beyond titles; deep vulnerability | Vulnerable to hurt pride and fears of rebellion (leader); fears of rejection or retaliation |

Within each role set, there come inherent strengths and weaknesses. The strengths can be built upon, developing a friendship and leader/follower relationship that enriches both people. The weaknesses need not necessarily occur—but it's helpful to name them and watch out for them. In Figure 2, I've included some of the inherent strengths and weaknesses of each role set. Take some time to look over that now.

As I mentioned before, I consider the easy development of trust and intimacy as strengths of this role set. I also mention jealousy, envy, and unhealthy competition as weaknesses. As friends who lead or follow those on the same hierarchical level, it can become easy to compare paths and achievements, honors, and failures. We are granted access into the vulnerabilities of these friends, and we tend to understand them best. We must take care to honor this information, and not fall prey to the human temptation to succeed at the expense of others.

## Role Set 2: Friends Leading Those Lower within the Hierarchical Structure

This role set looks like two friends at different levels in the hierarchy, with the friend higher in the organizational structure leading the friend lower in the organizational structure. As a leadership principle, this is the most common model, where a person leads someone lower in the organizational hierarchy. A boss leads a subordinate. The captain of the sports teams leads the other players. The general leads the troops. But as a friendship role set, fear keeps many leaders from befriending those under their official authority, a choice that will ultimately weaken their true leadership. To be effective, leaders must not distance themselves from people they would befriend lower in the hierarchical structure, or else they end up being unapproachable, demotivating, and weaker in their ability to influence. By bringing together natural leadership, hierarchical roles, and friendship, leaders will become more approachable, influential, stronger, and more compassionate. It is at this place maximum leadership and transformation is possible.

Figure 2 lists the strengths of this role set. As the natural leadership flows in the same direction as hierarchical structure, roles are more clearly defined and naturally align with the organization. Developing the friendship here would strengthen that already strong sense of leadership. In this context, however, the friend-follower will need to be aware of and possibly confront their fears of being manipulated or falling victim to power abuse, especially if they have experienced this before. A leader in this context may struggle with a fear of misplaced trust, betrayal, or outright rejection from those they lead. Though these fears may seem valid, they should not be accepted outright, but instead should be submitted to prayerful and thoughtful examination.

## Role Set 3: Friends Leading Those Above Them within the Hierarchical Structure

Finally, the last role set involves a friend in a lower hierarchical stratum leading a friend in a higher hierarchical stratum. While less common than the other two sets, these roles are demonstrated throughout the Bible as a powerful force of friendship. I have always been moved by the story in Second Samuel 12, where Nathan confronts David after the affair with Bathsheba. Though David was the highest formal authority in the kingdom, Nathan still approached his friend and king, bringing light to the darkness in his life. It was a painful circumstance with heart-breaking consequences, but still David responded to Nathan with sorrow and repentance. It was through Nathan's leadership in the life of David that David was able to make things right.

Personally, I have been encouraged, loved, challenged, and led by those under my official authority. It is humbling as my human pride wants to hide behind my position and title, but giving into that temptation would be foolish. God enjoys leading his children through unlikely sources, and refusing to allow my friends lower in the hierarchical system to influence and lead me is robbing them and myself of a God-given opportunity.

I've also experienced enriching friendships with those in authority over me—bosses who not only welcomed my friendship, but my input and leadership. They valued my influence in their life, and I valued their humility. Each relationship was a life-giving experience on all accounts.

When leadership is conducted in a healthy way, this role set cultivates an environment in which humble truth-telling is present. This strength allows for a broad respect to flourish, transcending titles, and a deep vulnerability to take root. Think of a time you've spoken humble truth in love to someone in authority over you—remember that moment of vulnerability, when you waited to see how they would respond? Or how about when someone under your authority came to speak to you in kindness and grace—remember the vulnerability you felt as you recognized their leadership in that moment? Accepting and walking in this role set, in appropriate measures, calls us toward the softening of hearts and spirits.

But this role set is not without its weaknesses. As leaders, we are vulnerable to our hurt pride and our own fears of rebellion. I remember being the leader of a mission team, and realizing there was a person on the team who was a stronger natural leader than I was. Initially, I felt insecure, worried they would wrestle power away from me and I would be forced to stand in the ashes of the chaos that they would rain down on the team. OK, that's a bit of an exaggeration. But I was worried every time they spoke up—would this be the moment they would challenge me in front of the whole team? After a couple days, my perspective shifted, however, as I took faith in the kind heart and gentle spirit of my friend who was helping to lead others along the path I had laid out. My fear of rebellion or conflict was only hurting me, and was ungenerous to the team member. It's always startling and disconcerting to realize a person under our authority is a naturally stronger leader, but this is no cause for fear.

Leaders are not the only ones who can struggle with fear in this role set. Many who are friends with their leaders can struggle with the fear of rejection ("What if they don't like what I say? What if they start to ignore me? What if I hurt them—will I lose my friend?") or retaliation ("As they are my boss, will this come back to hurt me professionally or personally? Is this going to show up on my performance review?").

In both of these instances, the fears of the leader and follower, proactive communication—sometimes *overcommunication*—is necessary as we grapple with our fears. Let our sensitivity to our friends guide our words and actions. And may we have grace in our lifelong journeys to recover from, and overcome, our weaknesses and fears.

The hope is that we would experience a diversity of relationships. Relationships with colleagues are not to be dismissed. They can be the place of some of a leader's strongest friendships. These kinds of friendships also must be carefully managed. Though they present the risks that accompany vulnerability, the dynamics of power are lessoned because it is a peer relationship. If friends live in other cities, it is easy for the relationship to provide very little actual encouragement, interaction, or relational intimacy. The friendship can quickly become more emotion-based and reliant on past memories rather than a current reality. Relationships that are challenged by geographical distance require intentional and regular communication in order to benefit the leader and to be relationships of influence.

It would be important not to limit the realm of friendship exclusively to colleagues. The ministry of Jesus modeled befriending others for the purpose of leadership development. They were the ones in whom he invested his life and entrusted the church. There should be those under the leader's realm of influence, with whom he or she likewise invests in at a personal level for leadership development. This deliberate investment in leaders, while nurturing friendship, creates a powerful atmosphere for influence and leadership development.

## Tips for Healthy Role Sets

By communicating through these role sets, each person is empowered to actively participate in the friendship. In every set, there are a few keys that will enable both follower and leader to work within the boundaries of their organizational role, while still enjoying the benefits of a thriving friendship.

1. *Keep Mutual Understanding.* Understanding the structural role of both people within the organizational hierarchy enables each person to embrace their work responsibilities, while maintaining a healthy friendship. A friend can receive direction from their boss when they have an understanding of their boss's role within the organization, as well as their own. Both should become familiar with each other's responsibilities and commitments, keeping these in mind as they communicate.

2. *Exercise Maturity.* Friendship between leaders and subordinates requires relational and emotional maturity in order to be successful. Emotions can get in the way of effectively accomplishing the workplace objectives. Is this the right place and time for certain conversations? For laughter or tears? When emotional maturity is lacking, the powerful dynamics of Friendship Leadership will break down, but a little circumspection can guide both friends as they navigate their roles.

3. *Pursue Balance.* There are dynamic tensions in all friendships. A good friendship requires balancing these forces. Some of these tensions include dependence and independence, acceptance and confrontation, assertiveness and disclosure. It requires balancing granting space and

showing commitment. A friendship is out of balance when a person has a level of intimacy and affection with another, which is not reciprocated. An unbalanced friendship can lead to frustration which will make itself known in both personal and professional arenas. No friendship is in perfect balance. There is no formula for keeping these things in balance, but communication is the necessary first step that can make an imbalanced relationship healthy again.

4. *Understand and Accept Varying Degrees of Friendship.* There are varying degrees of friendship: simply categorized, there are best friends, close friends, and casual friends. All of these friends are real and important, but in each case, the levels of commitment are different. Casual friends are real friends where "information is shared but it is rarely privileged."[8] The depth of intimacy with casual friends is less than it is with a close friend. Close friends are those who are important to each other and between whom a level of intimacy and self-disclosure exists. Time together is a requirement for keeping close friends close, as I mentioned in the qualities of friendship. Even when a feeling of closeness is maintained when time is not being invested in the relationship, those feelings are based on past memories, not the current relationship. This is why time together is so important. Best friends, are those with whom you share a high level of intimacy, usually including your "activities and relationships, your hopes, dreams, and fears."[9] They also are relationships of commitment or covenant. This creates strength and stability within friendship.

Consider the relationships you currently have that fall under the definition of Friendship Leadership. Can you describe your role? Your friend's role? Are there any underlying frustrations or fears about how the friendship is progressing? Could a little communication help ease some of that frustration? If a tension regarding roles *does* exist, I encourage you to step into that tension and communicate with your friend. In love and gentleness, you can reach a place where both are satisfied with the nature and boundaries of the roles you currently occupy, not encumbered by these roles, but freed through them to truly inhabit your friendship.

8. Yager, *Who's That Sitting At My Desk?*, 48.
9. Yager, *Who's That Sitting At My Desk?*, 48.

# PART 3

Empowering Friendship Leadership

# When Friendship Hurts

If an enemy were insulting me, I could endure it;

if a foe were rising against me, I could hide.

But it is you, a man like myself, my companion, my close friend,

with whom I once enjoyed sweet fellowship at the house of God,

as we walked about among the worshiper.

PSALM 55:12–14

## "The Cautionary Tale"

IF THERE WAS ONE piece of advice I absorbed as a young person entering the profession of pastoral leadership, it was this: don't become friends with people in your church. Weathered and worn, these older pastors and leaders were trying to save me from the heartbreak they had endured over the years. And they had the battle stories to accompany the warnings:

There was the pastor whose son was in a junior-high pop band with a church council member's son. When the band had a falling out, the council member (who had been a long-time family friend) led a churchwide rebellion against the senior pastor.

There was the pastor who became best friends with someone under their leadership, only to have that friend make a pass at the pastor's spouse. Feeling rejected, the friend then spread malicious rumors against the pastor's entire family.

There was the pastor who put up boundaries in regard to their home life, telling a friend they couldn't call at all hours of the day and night. That friend didn't choose to remain in the relationship much longer.

And what about the other side? When we befriend *our* leaders and they hurt us in devastating ways? These stories often include abuse of trust, gossip, inappropriate boundaries, and worse.

None of these stories are unfamiliar to you as you read through this chapter. In fact, you may have been holding your breath, anxiously waiting to read this chapter, because you already have a few stories of your own. Perhaps this narrative is unfortunately all too familiar. Your life has been the "cautionary tale," and you doubt Friendship Leadership can ever be redeemed. It is not my intention to diminish the risks of Friendship Leadership. I, too, have felt the pain that accompanies such a leadership philosophy. But I resolutely believe it is still worth it.

To begin with, let's name those risks, the fears lingering in the back of our hearts and minds. Proverbs 12:26 encourages the use of caution when establishing friendship, confirming that "a righteous man is cautious in friendship." An essential aspect of intentional Friendship Leadership includes examining the risks. If we were to pretend this process is "safety-guaranteed," we would be lying to ourselves and to each other.

As we go forward with the risks, let's keep this one vision in mind: that the church should be a place where people would be able to experience the proper fulfillment of the God-given desire for companionship and fellowship. Yet many parishioners and church leaders alike find themselves isolated. What risks contribute to this isolation and inhibit the development of Friendship Leadership?

## Risk 1: Vulnerability

One of the factors that stifles Friendship Leadership is the danger that exists when one becomes vulnerable with another person. Friendship involves taking a risk. It makes a person emotionally susceptible to suffering, disappointment, and loss. In my experience, many leaders avoid friendship altogether to avoid these possibilities. Instead, pastors have been urged by their peers and mentors to make friends outside the parish, preferably with peers who live in other cities, and leaders are encouraged to save friendship for their "off-time." This can create a very lonely existence. But what motivates this fear? Usually, it comes down to a few common things:

1. *We've Had Negative Experiences in the Past.* These usually involve hurt that has come out of friendships within the church or organization, which have left us wounded. As a leader, the potential for betrayal is real and is one of the biggest risks of friendship. This was a risk that Jesus took, even though he knew he would be betrayed.

   I've asked missionary and author, Jennifer Arimborgo, to share her experience in betrayal, which she notes as a common cultural occurrence in her context in the Peruvian Amazon. She shares this story with us:

> I began to mentor Sandrita when she was fifteen years old. She was among the first relationships I poured my heart and soul into when my husband, Israel, and I launched into full-time ministry time together. Though she lived outside of the city limits, Israel and I would make the forty-minute trek by motorcycle out to her house whenever she needed encouragement. I spent incalculable hours with her, ministering to her, praying with her, teaching her, discipling her. She was a key figure in my "first love" season of ministry.

> Sandrita confided in me that she had been conceived through rape, and that spiritual baggage she carried eventually took over her life. In time, hatred had grown up in her heart, spilling over into a vicious attack. She made up a vile story about Israel and let him know she planned on ruining him. She took it upon herself to systematically go throughout our entire church, visiting every home that would give her ear. She poured vehement zeal into realizing her goal of his destruction.

> Ten years have passed since then. Sandrita caused us a painfully prolonged season of heart wrenching trial. I have vivid memories of being curled in a fetal position, weeping from my very core and crying out to the Lord for His intervention. Eventually, the storm passed over. Our church only lost a handful of people over the ordeal. Just about everyone came to understand what a duplicitous person Sandrita had become and distanced themselves from her.

> Our scars were deep. However, I can honestly testify that the Lord has been indescribably close through the tears. The intimacy gained with Him through it all has been breathtaking. I have come to know His power and His love in a way that never would have

been possible without opening my heart to love the broken people that He died for.

I do not regret the years that I poured into Sandrita. Not in the tiniest way. Every moment that I gave to her, every bit of love from my heart, was unto the Lord. It was for Jesus. I continue to whole-heartedly thrive in full-time ministry. The Father regularly brings me more hurting children needing His touch. What if they later turn against me? I am not afraid. My heart says to Him, "Here I am Lord, send me!" I have learned from experience, no matter what I go through investing in relationship for His kingdom, He will faithfully, thoroughly, beautifully restore my soul.[1]

This story reminds us that all we have been through, and all we will yet endure, we do unto the Lord. We are called, and we respond. We worship through the way we persevere, even in the midst of pain and sorrow. We do not shut ourselves up with the pain, but instead, turn to the Lord for healing. In this way, He can prepare us, once again, to be open to friendship.

2. *We Fear Becoming Vulnerable.* This is especially true when it comes to opening up at a level of friendship, as it may cause people to lose respect for us—their leaders—when they realize we are just regular people. At times, this can be true—I've experienced the shock of people when they find out what kind of music I *really* listen to (no, it's not always the Christian pop radio station). I experience this most acutely on mission trips, when small groups of people are forced to live together for weeks at a time. They have the opportunity to see who I really am, what really annoys me, and where God is still molding me out of a big ol' lump of clay. The truth is, I can project a visage of perfection for two hours on a Sunday morning, but it's pretty hard to pull that off for weeks in a foreign country. In the end, they end up seeing the *real* me, weaknesses and strengths and all.

Instead of shirking back from this level of exposure, however, I press into the opportunity. It's a little awkward at first (*"Did my pastor really just say that?"*), but then we move into a deeper understand-ing of how God is working and extending grace to each of us. Only immature relationships require perfection. When we lead others into a friendship of vulnerability, we are giving them the opportunity to

1. Jennifer Arimborgo, in discussion with Matt Messner by phone, October 2017.

experience a deep and meaningful relationship—the kind Jesus offers. In the end, as we go through this process, people tend to gain respect for leaders when they become close to us.

3. *We Worry That Friendship Leadership May Result in Loss of Authority.* People who buy into this fear also follow the popular adage that effective leaders "lead from a distance." One Christian leader told me that this is important otherwise leaders lose their mystique and their ability to fill people's need for a hero. "If people really know me, they will not respect me," he stated, "People are looking for heroes and church leaders to fulfill this longing legitimately in a way that is motivating and inspiring." Yet, none of the research that I conducted verified this idea. On the contrary, the opposite is true: people are looking for leaders who are approachable and willing to walk beside them. The closer people get to a good leader, the greater their loyalty and the greater their respect. Dismissing this fear of a loss of respect, Pastor Jerry Cook shared with me his personal conviction that "Familiarity breeds contempt only for the contemptible."[2] As for the need to maintain the "mystique" of leadership, remember that God tore the temple veil in the Holy of Holies in order to become accessible and known. If God can be known, who are we to offer anything less? Are we more mysterious than God? More worthy of awe-filled distance? Of course not. We follow the example of the Creator-Friend who desires to be discovered.

The risk of vulnerability reveals to us two sides of the same fear: the fear of being let down, and the fear of letting others down. I have experienced both sides of this fear, as I'm sure you have, too. There have been times when those I counted as close friends rejected me, or leaders I trusted asked me to accomplish hard tasks. After all, friendship with other leaders is where we all stop being "heroes" and begin being humans. Although we know this to be true in theory, it doesn't minimize the pain we encounter when we are disappointed or hurt by someone we admire. Does this mean we avoid the process altogether? Absolutely not. If anything, when I consider how I've been let down by a leader and friend, I would say that it was the friendship itself that sustained the relationship. If we didn't have the foundation of friendship, the relationship would have dissolved, ceasing to exist. But because we had invested in friendship, the relationship was able to weather the storms of failure, disappointment, or misunderstanding.

2. Jerry Cook, in discussion with Matt Messner, June 2010.

Some of the closest and most long-lasting friendships in my life are testaments to what friendship can overcome.

Another way we experience disappointment is not through hurtful action, but by unavoidable separation. People move, they quit jobs, they finish school programs, they even die. For some people, these separations are the norm, like youth ministers, military families, or hospice workers. But everyone experiences this kind of disappointment over time, and it can tempt us into retreat. Your mind may ask you, "Why invest yourself in someone new, when they're just going to leave you like everyone else?" I'll be honest, this continual investment into the people who cross my path takes perseverance. I choose to intentionally remain open, looking for opportunities to forge friendship where it doesn't already exist. It's challenging—emotionally exhausting, sometimes—but I do it because I believe in this leadership principle.

My wife and I developed a family philosophy years ago. We believe that the only earthly thing we carry with us into eternity are relationships. Our friendships are eternal bonds. So no matter where life may take each of our friends, what separation moves us away from each other, we will remain open to the relationship. Each time we visit a city, we make it a priority to look up our friends. Even if we can't see everyone, we certainly try to set aside time to intentionally invest in that which lasts. People we haven't seen in years know they have an open invitation to stay with us whenever they roll through town, and we're delighted when they do. No friendship is relegated to "one chapter" of life; though the ways in which we communicate and spend time together may change, the friendship will always be there, as it is eternal. We may move onto other chapters in life, but we rejoice knowing that we bring our relationships with us, if not in person, then in our hearts. And we look forward to seeing our friends in Heaven, having all the time we desire to invest in each person. You could say this is our eschatological view of friendship. This celebration of relationship certainly sustains any disappointment we may feel on earth. So here and now, we do what we can to sustain friendships through separation (where possible), and remain open to the new friendships God provides.

More than when I'm disappointed, however, I experience pain when I let someone else down. As everyone I know will tell you—I am a bit of a perfectionist and hold myself to a high standard. I am deeply grieved when I disappoint others.

I remember staring numbly at my boss, who had just finished saying, "You know we have to make personnel cuts based on the budget. I need your help letting some staff members know that they need to go and find new jobs."

We were entering the holiday season and there couldn't have been a worst time to do this sort of thing.

My job responsibilities included providing the staff with support and oversight. They were my friends and I was deeply committed to each one of them. By striving to live out the ideals of Friendship Leadership, I had invested in them professionally and at a highly personal level. Now tasked with "firing my friends," I wished I didn't care so much. I knew that this action would wound them deeply and the anxiety led me to many sleepless nights.

Sitting across the table from one of my friends who was "being down-sized," I gave him the news as gently as possible. Earlier I had alluded to the fact that this might happen. Despite my efforts to soften the blow, he took it hard. He felt betrayed. I felt terrible. The depth of our friendship intensified the pain that we both felt.

He emotionally laid into me, his words cutting to my heart: "I thought we were friends? Friends don't do this to each other. This is the opposite of what friends do." I didn't know how to respond. I sat there in his pain and the emotion of the moment. I apologized and silently prayed for him.

I knew that our friendship had suffered a tremendous blow. I was not sure if it would ever recover. The hurt was very real but the presence of empathetic pain is a gauge that indicates the level of our emotional investment in another person. In moments like this, Jesus is the one who stands with friends even when they feel alone (both the leader and the subordinate). Experiencing this pain is one of the risks of being a leader who pursues friendship within hierarchical power structures.

I have been tempted to insulate myself from this kind of hurt by withdrawing emotionally. Many leaders have succumbed to this temptation, removing themselves from those whom they serve. If we give in, however, we will stifle our effectiveness and disconnect ourselves from the power of Friendship Leadership. As we go through the hurts of life, friendship is a glue that makes it possible to weather the storms that test the relationships that are most important to us.

It is in these moments I rely on the grace of God. This is where the theoretical moves into the actual, and I find grace isn't just a "good idea," but something I desperately need—to receive and to give. And denying someone my vulnerability will not protect them from me—it will only isolate both of us, a reality far more harmful to both of us in the long run.

Decisions leading to the isolation of the leader creep in as a conscious or unconscious defense mechanism. Isolation keeps a person at a safe distance from the hurt of close relationships. Yet the ethical fallacy of these defense mechanisms lies in the fact that they have been elevated above the scriptural mandates to love. For many Christian leaders, these fears and mechanisms have superseded the greatest commandments to love God and to love our neighbor. How is it possible to love God and to love people without being open to caring relationships and friendships?

Friendship Leadership cannot be ruled out because one fears being truly known. The greatest risk of friendship is that its main expression is love. To love people is to become vulnerable. And when one is vulnerable there is the potential to be hurt. Especially in its early stages, friendship includes the legitimate fear of being hurt. As trust increases, this fear becomes less conscious. Betrayal is a great risk in any friendship, and conflict can lead to the deterioration of a friendship and an ultimate loss. If we look to Jesus as our example, we can see that he was hurt countless times, and if it happened to him, it will happen to us. This is the price we pay to follow in his footsteps.

He promises, however, that we don't have to endure alone. We have a Friend who is carrying us while we invest in our earthly friends. We believe that he also can supply the grace and forgiveness needed to navigate through the hurt. In this way, we remain soft-hearted, open and available. Not without risk, but in spite of it.

## Risk 2: Preferential Love

Meilaender, in his book, *Friendship: A Study in Theological Ethics*,[3] outlines several of the ethical challenges that can arise from the pursuit of friendship. One is that friendship, by its very nature, demonstrates "preferential love." In other words, having friends implies the exclusion of others. This creates an insider/outsider dichotomy. Aristotle's writings on friendship struggled with this reality, and concluded that "to be friends with many people, in the sense of perfect friendship, is impossible."[4] The preferen-

3. Meilaender, *Friendship*.

4. Aristotle, *Nicomachaen Ethics*, 149.

tial nature of friendship reinforces the fact that one's ability to be friends with everyone is unrealistic. Although one can be friendly to just about everyone, the number of close friendships a person can support is limited. This issue was addressed under the "Priority" section in chapter 4, and the risk of preference inhibits some attempting friendship at all.

It is because of the preferential nature of friendship that groups of close friends are often perceived in a negative way as cliques. They are considered to be exclusive or closed-off. Groups of friends can unknowingly project a sense of "insiders and outsiders." It creates, to those who are not a part of the circle of friends, a chasm of separation. This pride over friendship can cast a negative impression on those who do not share in the experience of friendship. This is an ethical issue for friends to be aware of, sensitive to, and careful about.

In my own life, I try to mediate these negative effects of friendship. I believe those engaged in Friendship Leadership should exercise a high level of professionalism in the workplace or organization. In the time we're working to accomplish the vision of the organization or business, deepening our friendship is not the primary goal. Most of the personal friendship dynamics should happen outside the workplace. Truthfully, everyone at work knows a leader can only have a limited number of friends (especially in a large organization), but we don't have to show off our close friendships in front of the public. So we limit the inside jokes, the weekend plans or recaps to conversations outside of work. Engaging in those behaviors inside the workplace shows an insensitivity to the feelings of others. Such insensitivity will hurt others, make some feel uncomfortable, and inevitably result in an insider/outsider tone. While at work, I also try to find ways to include others in the social things I do during work hours (e.g. inviting others to lunch). It can be a simple, easy gesture, but it demonstrates inclusivity.

We also never know if those outside the "inner circle" might eventually move into the inner circle of our lives. There are cycles of friendships, so we keep the doors open in our lives. If our actions demonstrate an insensitive exclusivity, it could cause long-lasting damage, impeding any future opportunities for Friendship Leadership to arise. Here's how to know if you have a healthy circle of friendships, or if you've created an unhealthy clique: imagine all your closest friends move away tomorrow—are there other people who would be open to friendship with you? Or have you burned all those bridges? This risk of preferential love needn't be debilitating, but it does require a thoughtful expression of Friendship Leadership.

Furthermore, the risk of "preferential love" can unearth our own fear of rejection. Perhaps you've opened the door to friendship with someone, and they closed that door in your face, choosing someone else instead. How do we stay open to relationship when we've been spurned, overlooked, or excluded? We begin by understanding that these feelings reveal our own longing for intimacy and inclusion. They are a sign in our lives that some emotional need isn't being met. Through contemplative prayer, we can bring these deeper issues to light and to God. As a result, it becomes an opportunity to develop empathy. This feeling of rejection can either harden our hearts against friendship or soften our hearts toward a more inclusive and accepting form of friendship.

As we look outside ourselves, we can make sure we don't cause anyone else to feel that way. Look around you—is there some initiative you can take with someone else who may be feeling that way? You can join up with them. Within my professional networks, when I find I'm overlooked in one area of relational opportunity, I find there are other opportunities awaiting me in a different area, possibly with other people who feel the same way I do. I can still do good in my circles of influence; my leadership and vision aren't impeded by the choices or rejections of others. More than that, I can be the difference I want to experience for myself. For example, when I attend conferences with hundreds, even thousands, of attendees, I will consciously look for those who might be excluded, the person sitting alone during lunch breaks, or heading back to the hotel early. This is a rare opportunity to invest in people we don't often get to see, to build friendships with those outside my normal sphere of Friendship Leadership. It's a chance to be inclusive.

As we face this risk of preferential love, I cannot stress enough the importance of communication. If you would like to invest time in a friendship, make sure that's communicated to your friend. If you feel hurt or rejected by someone, give them the opportunity to hear you out and possibly explain their actions. If someone has accused you of creating an "insider/outsider" scenario, receive it with grace and an open mind, remembering that they, too, are carrying the burdens of past rejections and insecurities. If you have a limited time to invest in a friendship, take the initiative to communicate with your friends—don't make them come to you wondering where you've been; own up to your limits from the get-go.

Finally, express your boundaries clearly. As a pastor, I feel that many members of the congregation can hold a certain perception of intimacy with me that is not reciprocal. This is completely understandable because I share the deepest issues of life with them through sermons every weekend. They hear about me, my struggles, my victories, my fears, and my celebrations. They care for me and my family in a way that is unique to the role I fill. While this care is appreciated, it can sometimes result in a one-sided friendship dynamic, where they can expect more of me than I may be able to give. Instead of shying away from this reality—my own limitations—I try to express what I am actually capable of doing. I've even known some pastors who shared their boundaries through a sermon from the pulpit. While I've never personally done this, if it would serve you and those under your leadership best, then I encourage you to consider creative ways to present your honest boundaries. This communication can keep our natural human limitations from appearing as personal slights or rejections. While this isn't foolproof, it can cover a multitude of shortcomings.

## Risk 3: Blindness

Another risk of friendship is that strong friendships can sometimes blind a leader from reality. Friends will either be the ones who inspire leaders to greatness, or who bring them down. "It [friendship] makes good men better and bad men worse."[5] It can create a deafness to outside opinion, "a vacuum across which no voice will carry."[6] Friends are so persuasive that what a friend thinks may carry more weight than a thousand others. Many leaders have blindly held onto the opinion of their hand-selected inner circle—the "yes men" who will only agree with them. Love is blind, and even the love of friendship can be blinding to reality. Friends' opinions and their shared influence can be a positive motivator, or it can be the voice that leads a person to their grave. Lewis reminds us that "every real Friendship is a sort of secession, even a rebellion."[7] This is why the vision, the character, and the heart of a friend must be carefully considered.

Though our disproportionate focus on the opinions of friends can lead to blindness if not managed well, the understanding of our key influencers can actually be a tool to motivate and inspire, if we proceed with wisdom. Here's one such example:

5. Lewis, *The Four Loves*, 82.

6. Lewis, *The Four Loves*, 82.

7. Lewis, *The Four Loves*, 82.

When I was in high school, I was all-too-aware of my own suscep-
tibility to peer pressure. I really cared what my friends thought,
much more so than my parents or teachers. I also was only just
managing to pass my classes, even though I knew I could do better. So when the time came to graduate and move on to college, I
decided I would use peer pressure for my own advantage.

From the first day of college, I befriended the smartest kids in
each class. All of my friends were pulling straight As in advanced
classes. And if I was going to "fit in," I knew I needed to keep up. I
remember walking into chemistry class, and my friend asking how
the homework had gone the previous night. I can remember the
horror on her face when I said, "Oh, I didn't do the homework. I
went to the movies instead." She was disappointed in me, and that
meant far more than the disappointment of anyone else. I quickly
shaped up and became a straight A student myself. I wasn't a victim
of peer pressure; I had known instinctively that my friends held an
influence over me, but by selecting the right friends, I could make
sure that influence pointed me in a direction I wanted to go.

Though we were all warned the dangers of "peer pressure" growing
up, we don't necessarily continue to receive those same warnings as adults,
do we? Yet we remain susceptible to the risks of blindness throughout our
lives. Friendship Leadership can only be as healthy as the people participat-
ing, so choose your levels of influence and intimacy carefully. The risk of
blindness can be mediated through thoughtful selection. It reminds us of
the importance of not becoming so exclusive in friendship that we fail to
hear, or listen to, the advice of others.

Does this mean that the risks of friendship are too great? Actually,
these are necessary risks. A *greater* blindness to reality exists when one does
not love. It exists when one lives in isolation and avoidance of relationships.
Only a friend really understands and appreciates the heart of a friend. Their
love actually frees them from the blindness that exists in relationships that
lack a caring knowledge of each other.

The question has been asked, "Why is it that we reserve our worst
behavior for those we love the most?" Although this is often the case in
families, it also can be true in friendships. One of the risks of getting close
to someone is the increasing potential for disputes. Friendship Leadership
is an arena of great emotional fragility, vulnerability, and expression. Good
relational skills keep friendships intact, enabling one to handle conflict
maturely, with grace, forgiveness, and unconditional love. Reconciliation,

humility, and restitution are aspects of friendship that need to be exercised. In a healthy friendship, it is love that covers over a multitude of sins. Friendship that influences and endures these risks requires the emotional maturity that Emerson described here: "Our friendships hurry to short and poor conclusions, because we have made them a texture of wine and dreams, instead of the tough fiber of the human heart."[8]

With all of the risks, why advocate the development of Friendship Leadership? Why take these risks? For those in the world, the risks may outweigh the benefits. A leader can choose to keep "a healthy distance" from those they lead. But in the kingdom of God, fear must not be the motivation and basis for action. Instead, actions should be carried out on the basis of love and the mandate of Scripture. This must be a journey of faith, for faith in man is essential to faith in God. Faith is expressed in the risks of friendship.

The risks of friendship are real, but none are so insurmountable as to preclude friendship altogether. Risks offer the leader serious practical considerations when considering the role of friendship in leadership, but these do not negate the power nor the priority that friendship can have. Take some time to review your story with Friendship Leadership, answering the discussion questions honestly. Allow your heart some time to grieve, to mourn, to express fear and failure. Name the risks, and then confront them. Remember, you are not alone in the risk-taking; there is a Friend who continues to take risks on your behalf, and who strengthens you as you courageously and humbly consider Friendship Leadership.

8. Stade, *Essays and Poems*, 176.

# 8

## Dual Relationships

"AS A PASTOR YOU must avoid having dual relationships. It is an issue of professional ethics." My seminary professor drilled this into us during our class, Pastoral Counseling. This mandate left me puzzled and conflicted. How could I lead people and not have dual relationships? Friendship Leadership is a highly relational way of leading and it is not confined to a professional environment. As a youth pastor, I had invested in the kids I served by going to their school activities, having meals with them, playing sports, watching movies, and "sharing life" together. I had been taught, "They will not care what you know until they know that you care." A very personal approach to ministry and discipleship had shaped my life and seemed rooted in the way Jesus led his own disciples. So why the prohibition?

Dual relationships are those where a leader "assumes two roles simultaneously or sequentially with a person or persons engaging their professional assistance."[1] For instance, a person can have a dual relationship when he or she conducts a professional counseling session with a client and then plays on a city league softball team with that same person. Counselors and psychologists are required to keep strict boundaries regarding their relationships with their clients. In some of these contexts, nurturing a friendship with one's own client is considered unethical. Pastors and other leaders have followed suit by adopting this approach. "Pastors often struggle with these issues [dual relationships]and often do so without clear professional boundaries that assist traditional psychotherapists in avoiding dual relationships."[2] Consequently, training in Pastoral Care has come to

1. Sanders, *Christian Counseling Ethics*, 53.
2. Sanders, *Christian Counseling Ethics*, 53.

incorporate avoidance of dual relationships. The American Psychological Association has warned professional counselors and psychologists that they should avoid these relationships because they can "impair the psychologist's objectivity or otherwise interfere with the psychologist effectively performing his or her functions as a psychologist, or might harm or exploit the other party."[3]

At the heart of the issue of dual relationships is a valid concern designed to protect both the client and the professional caregiver. Some people have difficulty understanding and respecting appropriate boundaries, so guidelines such as this have to be established. The following case study was written by a counselor and provides an example of the blurring of boundaries between roles of leadership (in this case—professional responsibility) and friendship:

> My relationship with Heather began professionally and we went to things professionally. Then she began to call me a lot; I mean I liked her. She was nice. The problem with Heather for me was that Heather is a smothering person to be a friend with, and Heather likes to possess you and Heather wants to control you—she's not rude about it, you understand, but she wants you to do it her way, and she wants it to be her idea, and she wants that in a friendship, not just professionally and not just in a classroom. And I guess I didn't realize how intensely awful I resented that until we were finally in the same building together and I felt like she was running my life. And I think I resented her a lot because on the one hand, I liked her as a person, but I hated working with her, just hated it. I couldn't come to terms with liking her as a person and hating to work with her."[4]

In cases like this, people tend to alter their roles to become more strictly professionally-based, or friendship-based. Complex dynamics of personality, roles, power, expectations, and boundaries all contribute to the unique and challenging dynamics that sometimes play into friendships where dual roles exist. It's one thing to reach out to a needy person, but it's another to have a friendship.

Leaders will go through times of emotional neediness where the temptation exists to have those needs met through followers or subordinates. Instead, leaders must look elsewhere to have those needs met in a healthy

---

3. American Psychological Association. "Ethical Principles of Psychologists and Code of Conduct." (Section 1.17). https://www.apa.org/ethics/code/code-1992.aspx.

4. Williams, *Friendship Matters*, 206.

way, outside the leadership role they occupy. A good leader knows their role is about fulfilling the organization's mission, not having their personal and emotional needs met.

Caution is necessary whenever there is an imbalance of power in a relationship. Spiritual abuse, sexual abuse, harassment, and favoritism are all expressions of toxic dual relationships. It is important for a leader to recognize their limits. It is helpful to remember that even though Jesus reached out to thousands of people, He was selective about developing strong relationships with only a few. Since dual relationships by definition blur boundaries between different interpersonal roles, these problems are likely to become more severe when either person in the friendship has difficulty maintaining boundaries in the first place.

These realities should not rule out the possibility of friendship within the context of the church and church leadership. Healthy friendships respect boundaries, take productive risks, avoid manipulation, and remain free from pathological tendencies. Unfortunately, not all leaders have the relational skills needed to keep friendships healthy.

Another motivating factor behind the avoidance of "dual relationships" in the helping professions is a fear of litigation. How do you grow close to people without becoming a target? Counselors have had to establish boundaries to protect themselves professionally. Many church leaders have also done this for the very same reason. Whenever this happens, fear has become a higher value and motivating factor than love.

Being so fear-driven that a person disregards the biblical model and mandate to love, is to lose sight of something essentially important, and greatly inhibits the effectiveness of leaders. By overemphasizing an avoidance of dual relationships, leaders become increasingly isolated and out of touch, giving up the cutting edge of their leadership potential. Instead, may we exercise self-care, self-awareness, and accountability. These are important safeguards against unethical dual relationships.

We cannot live in community without the existence of dual relationships. Instead of hiding behind a misplaced ethic, live the mandate to "Love your neighbor as yourself."

## 9

# Friendship Leadership in High Power Distance Cultures

"I'D LOVE TO BE friends with my subordinates, but it is literally prohibited in my line of work." A Coast Guard officer (and friend of mine) was explaining to me why Friendship Leadership was challenging in his context. "I could get in trouble just for inviting one of my enlisted subordinates to a BBQ at my house after hours."

A common barrier to Friendship Leadership is found in our external context, in the cultures in which we live and work. While some environments may be more conducive to relationships of vulnerability and mutual care, others present a conflict when the distance between leader/follower or boss/subordinate is perceived as impassable. We will refer to these contexts as "high power distance" cultures.

Power distance is the space between tiers of a hierarchical structure. More than that, it also applies to how that space is *perceived*. Do the people within the culture believe some have more power than others? Is everyone comfortable with this distribution of power? How do people at differing levels of power interact—what is allowed, appropriate, and encouraged?

Sometimes, these questions are answered through the unspoken passing down of tradition (e.g. "That's just the way it's done"). Other times, they are reinforced through language and action (e.g. "You must address him/her by their title"). Finally, in some contexts, the answers to these questions are formally written out, as a method of maintaining correct action in a given environment (e.g. a Code of Conduct stipulating appropriate behavior).

In this chapter, we will consider Friendship Leadership within two specific high power distance cultures: corporate culture and societal culture. The purpose isn't to undermine the cultures in which we live and work, but rather to seek a creative and biblical response to these contexts. As we submit to our calling in a given place, how can we achieve the Christ-likeness that can only be demonstrated through Friendship Leadership?

## Introduction to Power Distance

Several studies have been conducted over the years to identify and describe the power distance within given contexts. For the purpose of their study, the Globe research team defined power distance as "the degree to which members of an organization expect and agree that power should be shared unequally."[1] In his research, Hofstede defined high power distance as "the extent to which less powerful members of institutions and organizations within a country expect and accept that power is distributed unequally."[2] And Plueddemann writes that: "In high-power-distance cultures both leaders and followers assume that the leader has more authority, respect and status symbols. The leader has the right to make unilateral decisions that will be obeyed without question. In these societies, employees do not question managers, students do not challenge teachers, and children obey parents or other elders without question."[3]

In other words, the two elements of a high power distance culture are that 1) power is distributed unequally, and 2) all/most participants in the culture agree that this is acceptable. Every church/organization/family/society exists somewhere on the high-to-low power distance spectrum. It's important to be able to identify your context's placement on the spectrum to thoughtfully engage in Friendship Leadership.

As a jumping off point, ask yourself:

- How are decisions made? Is it one individual or a team? If the group doesn't approve of the decision, is there a method or means of challenging the decision?

- What is the prevalence of egalitarian relationships? Are the persons in a relationship mostly interacting from uneven power placements or are most interacting from a place of equal footing?

1. Robert, *Culture, Leadership and Organizations*, 517.

2. Hofstede, *Cultures and Organizations*, 46.

3. Plueddemann, *Leading Across Cultures*, 94.

- How often do people agree to enact a decision for the reason: "Because he/she is the boss, and they told us to do it"? Or, "I'm just following orders"?

- How is status identified? Through titles? Clothes? Perks of the position? Degrees held? Is it possible to identify a person's power distance merely by watching their interactions with others?

- How challenging is it to acquire more power within your context? Is it mainly shared by a small group at the top of a vertical hierarchy, or is it shared throughout a more horizontal hierarchy?

- Finally, do most seem to approve of the stratified power distribution? Is it understood as a method for creating order and necessary to the success of the organization or society?

- These are just a few of the questions that can guide us toward understanding our context better.

Perhaps the context is even bigger than we realize. In some cases, the interactions of an intimate office setting may indicate a low power distance model, but the organization as a whole interacts with other organizations through a high power distance. Plueddemann describes what this might look like.[4] Though he is referencing churches, it is equally applicable in organization structures. In church partnership settings, high power distance can be identified thus:

- In church partnerships, there must always be a "senior" church and a "junior" church.

- When it comes to sharing resources, both churches are most comfortable with assuming either a "patron" or "client" position.

- In missions settings, either the missionary (coming from a high power distance culture) or the mission project (existing in a high power distance culture) will expect the missionary to stay in a place of high power for a long time.

- The most important decisions are expected to be made by the people at the top of the hierarchical structure.

These considerations can also reveal our personal biases, a fact that is especially important when we are working cross-culturally. There are

4. Plueddemann, *Leading Across Cultures*, 103.

a number of ways to categorize cultural barriers we may cross: socioeconomic, racial, linguistic, etc. The way we were brought up, the way we've been taught to understand the world, informs our approach to Friendship Leadership. Perhaps when you read the questions and descriptions above, you noticed a personal reaction within yourself (e.g. "This isn't how my workplace is, but it's how it *should* be," or, "Of course this is true in my workplace. It's the most appropriate way to engage"). I encourage you to take note of any knee-jerk reaction to either side of the power distance spectrum; it could be a clue as to where you personally fall, and will color the way you interact with the context around you.

Let me give you an example from a missionary friend:

> I was once working in a South American church project, on a team comprised of both American and local church leaders. As we worked together, I grew uncomfortable with the high power distance present within the organizational structure, where those "at the top" possessed the majority of the power, and that power was obeyed without hesitation. It was a system expected by the leaders and approved of by the followers. Though, as an American, I was placed higher up in the hierarchy, I was still hesitant about the situation as a whole.
>
> After a few weeks, I approached another American missionary who had been serving in that context for years. I relayed my discomfiture, to which, he responded, "That's because you're American."
>
> I immediately responded, "But so are you!"
>
> "Yes," he agreed. "But I can see both sides. They are accustomed to the hierarchy here, while you are accustomed to an American idea of egalitarianism."
>
> I realized that he was right. My friend wasn't making an argument for or against high power structures, merely helping me see that my own perspective was getting in my way of effective leadership.[5]

As my missionary friend shared, I would encourage you to be aware not only of your context, but of your own feelings regarding what is "right"

5. Rachel McMurray-Branscombe, in email discussion with the Matt Messner, March 2017.

and "appropriate." They may affect your ability to work within Friendship Leadership more than you know.

Though Friendship Leadership is easier to establish and maintain in a low power distance culture, the purpose of this section isn't to condemn high power distance cultures. There are other resources available that can dive into the pros and cons of high/low power distance. Even within the biblical text, there are examples on both sides of the spectrum—within the person of God, who is the almighty, unquestioned Creator and ruler, but is also our friend, lowering himself to become like us. So the question becomes, how can we engage lovingly within a cultural context that maintains distance between levels of power?

## Corporate culture

I believe this philosophy of leadership has the ability to transcend the lines that separate a Christian organization from a secular workplace environment. And yet, I also know that because of these lines, leaders working in modern-day corporate culture will need to find creative and authentic ways to live out their values. For some of you, Friendship Leadership could be challenging to integrate, especially if you find yourself in a cut-throat, dog-eat-dog structure. But I think we are finally starting to realize, as a society, that people need relational connection, encouragement, and a sense of "belonging to something bigger" at work. Friendship Leadership, though founded on biblical examples, speaks to the greatest need of every human in every workplace: the need to be seen, heard, understood, and loved. This remains true, even where strict hierarchical structures clearly delineate roles and positions, bringing the relevance of Friendship Leadership to the forefront of this conversation.

Consider the modern U.S. military. In addition to having a high power distance, it is also an example of a strong grid culture: one in which the roles are clearly defined, with members staying within the boundaries of their precise role in the organization. Roles are not interchangeable. Lingenfelter writes:

> The idea of grid focuses on how people in a social game categorize individual players by distinctive positions and roles. The more numerous and specialized the positions of players and the greater the performance restriction . . . the stronger the grid. More social distinctions usually imply more sharply defined expectations

and social rules. The larger the number of rules, the greater the constraints upon individuals in the structuring of social relationships; managers do not socialize with players, and presidents of companies do not socialize with laborers."[6]

When a context combines a high power distance with a strong grid, an intentional leader is required to implement Friendship Leadership. As I was writing this book, I knew I wanted to interview a friend serving in the U.S. Air Force, Captain Boston McClain, who always makes relationships a priority, no matter the context.

To explain the hierarchical system of the U.S. Air Force, McClain briefly explained the roles of the enlisted ("worker bees," and often the tech specialists) and the officers, where the higher one goes in rank, the less they are specialists, and instead have a broad managerial knowledge. This ranking structure provides a systematic hierarchy. Perhaps your workplace isn't as clearly defined, but many organizations and businesses have their own "ranking" system—and the higher one goes, the more they shift from task-based work to management. A corporate culture with an emphasis on hierarchy can feel confining to the preclusion of the Friendship Leadership model. To discuss this more, Captain McClain shares these responses with us:[7]

- Is it possible for a person to lead from a place of friendship, while still observing the corporate culture in which they work?

  Yes! I would recommend you emphasize the qualities of friendship most available to you. For me, in a military corporate structure, that quality is respect. Respect is emphasized in the very oath that military members take: "to obey the lawful orders of those appointed over us." For someone in the military, the presence (or absence) of respect can have life-threatening consequences.

  *(Author's note: What are the natural qualities of friendship found within your workplace that you can build upon? Is loyalty a value of your organization? Or time investment? Perhaps not every quality is available to you at first, but look for the small ways to build up friendship through the values already embedded within your organization.)*

---

6. Lingenfelter, *Transforming Culture*, 192.

7. Boston McClain, in videochat discussion with Rachel McMurray-Branscombe, December 2017.

As for the specific role sets, engaging in Friendship Leadership with peers can be both the easiest and the hardest. If you are leading a person with your same beliefs, then it's easy to connect as friends. But if you have to lead a peer who isn't on the same page with values and morals, you can have a hard time investing in this friendship. But I make a conscious decision to overwhelm this person with positivity, to give space while still communicating I see their value.

When I build friendships with those I lead, yes, they must respect the role I fill. But I must respect them, because if our relationship lacks respect, then friendship can't exist. People want to be loved and respected, and I can do this across hierarchical lines. When I willingly offer this love and respect, I know that they follow my leadership even more—there is purpose and they believe in me, as I believe in them.

Finally, when I build friendships with those in leadership over me, I have to watch my own heart and motivations. I'm a Type A and goal-oriented leader, and so I can't help but feel competitive with others, which, if I'm not vigilant, can create an environment for pride and jealousy to creep in. But if I'm truly friends with these leaders, then not only do I respect their positional leadership, but I respect them because of our friendship. So I choose to focus on God and focus on the friendship, because that's what really matters.

- Do you find your corporate culture limits your ability to practice Friendship Leadership?

  While the military discourages "unprofessional relationships" between officers and enlisted members, for me, the "unprofessional" aspect derives from showing preference or favoritism. I follow the rules, but my values inform *how* I live out those rules. I believe I can follow the mandates of my corporate structure while still allowing the value of relational leadership to color my choices. Everyone, even tough people in the military, need others to love and respect them.

  I try to be intentional. In the workplace, I go around to every shop and greet every person. It takes me about thirty to forty-five minutes every morning, but it helps me get to know everyone. At first, they always asked, "What do you need?" But I would respond, "I just want to say hello." And now they expect the visit—they know I want to see how they're doing. It can even be small gestures, like remembering a birthday or smiling at coworkers. People may be initially thrown off or suspicious, but time and consistency will show these actions are genuine and not an act. In this way, you can cultivate friendships that wouldn't normally happen. It doesn't take a lot of effort, but it allows me to build up friendships while in the workplace, and then anything that happens outside work, happens in fertile soil of relationship.

- What advice would you give someone who works within a rigid system, but still wants to lead out of a place of caring?

    I find it's actually less exhausting to lead through friendship because you're living life to the fullest. Instead of a bunch of little pieces of who I am—husband, father, Christian, coworker—with each needing time and resources, I can reconcile all that through real relationships. Leadership becomes a lot easier then, as everything in life is working toward one common purpose and mission.

    Also, remember that you never know where someone is in life. A few weeks ago, there was an airman who committed suicide. So how do we, in their community, process that? What was going on in their head? They must have felt very alone. There's so much more to life than just working, and so if someone merely shows up and does the job, they miss they chance to go a little deeper. It could make a real impact on someone's life. Leadership is not just living our lives to the fullest, but helping others live theirs.

    Finally, I think we have to fight the cultural norms of Western society, or be mindful of them, which has evolved into a money-driven, individualistic society, based off personal happiness. Ask any person: "When have you felt at your lowest? When did you make your worst choice?" I bet it was when they were feeling alone. Suicide, illegal activity, overdosing on pills, drinking and driving— each of these actions has loneliness buried within them. Instead of being reclusive, we need to turn outward and look for our strength within other people.

    (Author's note: this is why we encourage Friendship Leadership; it presents a foil to the dangerous narrative of the reclusive and lonely leader.)

- How do you prepare internally to bring Friendship Leadership into a non-Christian setting?

It takes quite a bit of intentionality. Every morning, I sit in my car and pray for words and opportunities. As an act of humility, I pray to die to myself and live for God. My day is not about me; it's about other people. It's not about what I want to accomplish; my role is to build others up. Even when I don't feel like it, I engage in the task of Friendship Leadership and build the "muscle memory" of humility. It's working out the muscle of person-oriented leadership.

I try to focus on the things I can't always quantify. I embrace every day for what it brings—practicing mindfulness to remember the prioritization of relationships. I am where I'm supposed to be—right here, and right now. This takes spiritual discipline. When I'm not in sync with God or not focused, these can be very challenging.

Additionally, I find other healthy outlets in my workplace. I look for a friend who is similar to me in values and perspective. I need these people to talk to throughout the day, as we can offer each other encouragement from a place of understanding.

Finally, I understand the implications of my actions. When I say, "I'm going to be a light for God's kingdom," but I melt down in anger, what are the far-reaching implications of that? I don't take this responsibility of relational leadership lightly. There is a gravity to Christian leadership. I'm not selling Jesus, I'm supposed to be like Jesus, who prioritized the relationships in his leadership.

For Captain McClain, the way he chooses to lead affects not only his work outcomes, but the very lives and safety of the people with whom he serves. And within his high power distance corporate culture, McClain sees the value and tangible results of utilizing Friendship Leadership. Now, let's look at another type of culture.

## Societal culture

Missions and cross-cultural workers are always at the forefront of my mind when I consider Christian leadership. Gone are the days when leadership models only had to work for a homogeneous community—as we seek to live out the Great Commission while our global networks are expanding at an exponential pace, our models need to account for sociocultural differences. For that reason, let's look at how Friendship Leadership could be lived out in a culture different than the western Christian protestant context from which I write and lead.

Hofstede created a helpful index that ranks countries and their comparative power distance This index will be a generalization and is not meant to be conclusive, but rather, a jumping-off point. Not surprisingly, the United States holds a mid-level power distance index level of forty, low compared to Mexico's eighty-one or Malaysia's 104. But even the U.S. has a high score when one looks at New Zealand's twenty-two. This index has now been made available through Hofstede Insights,[8] so cross-cultural workers can get a sense of how their perspective on leadership, power, roles, and relationships are affected by context.

But let's bring these numbers to life. I asked another missionary friend to include their experience here:

> Being from the Pacific Northwest region of the U.S., I like to usually keep things "casual." When people address me, I prefer they leave off the "Pastor So-and-so" title. I want to be relatable and lead from a place of egalitarian friendship and camaraderie. So when I moved to the mission field, I had some challenges adjusting to the new culture.
>
> To begin with, everyone insisted on using my title. There was a reverence for my role, and by substitution, me. All advice was expected to go only one direction—from me (the pastor) to them (the congregant). If I needed advice myself, or was just feeling a little weak, there was an understanding that I shouldn't look for support within the congregation of the church. This was indeed a far cry from my home context!
>
> At first, I tried to adopt the serious and somber facade I thought I was expected to wear. I kept the barriers up between leaders and subordinates, my passion and humanity revealed only once a week in my Sunday sermon. But I could feel a loneliness creeping in. I had my friends back at home, but they didn't really understand my struggles (not to mention the fact that many missionaries feel they have to hide their struggles for fundraising purposes.) Some missionaries work in a context with others from their home country, but that wasn't my case. It was just me, the missionary, and the people I was there to serve.

8.  Hofstede,    *Country    Comparisons,*    www.hofstede-insights.com/
country-comparison/.

Finally, I couldn't take the solitude any more. I decided that I would make a friend. With great trepidation, I found a like-minded person within the church, someone who had proven trustworthy and with whom I shared a common interest: music. We began to meet together to play music, sometimes bringing out a guitar or drum; other times, just listening to recordings of some local music. In this way, we slowly began to build a friendship. I knew it would never look like how friendships looked back at home, but it still had all the basic elements of friendship: there was love, respect, and humanity. I was able to know them, and they were able to know me better.

I think that's the thing cross-cultural workers can forget, sometimes. We work so hard to know and understand the people whom we are serving we can forget that we, too, need to be known and understood. We may have to adapt the process based on the culture, but friendship as a cross-cultural leader is a possibility. Look for common ground, speak to the deepest need of being heard and known, and go from there.[9]

I would like to think a cross-cultural worker doesn't need to choose between Friendship Leadership and respecting the local culture of their context. Let's return to the markers of friendship that informed our definitions back in chapter 3. Isaacs identified friendship as demonstrating mutuality, volition, interdependence, and care.[10] Even within a high power distance culture, two people can both choose to enter into a relationship in which they rely on each other and care for one another. Sometimes, the interdependence isn't demonstrated through an egalitarian sharing of power, but rather a trust that each person within the hierarchy will perform their mission with success and integrity. This type of trust *is* a form of interdependence, though unfamiliar or possibly uncomfortable to those from cultures raised to question or second-guess authority.

And the passage in John 15:13–15 emphasizes friendships of love, sacrifice, and disclosure. If any of those markers are more challenging in a high power distance culture, perhaps it would be "disclosure." Even in your home culture, however, you innately discern where, how, and with whom to disclose certain parts of your life (e.g. which information is appropriate for your small group and what should be reserved for an accountability

9. Rachel McMurray-Branscombe, in email discussion with Matt Messner, June 2018.

10. Isaacs, *Toxic Friends, True Friends*, 210.

partner). The same practice is applied here—look for the appropriate people for disclosure, investing in those friendships even as you lead.

This leadership model isn't about changing the culture of your context, either corporate or societal (much damage has been done by Christian leaders trying to "fix" their host cultures). Instead, it's about learning to understand the culture, and see how you can allow your values and perspective on leadership to infuse your actions. As it is, I like to think of Jesus as our ultimate cross-cultural leader—he who became like us, and leads us through his offer of friendship.

## Cross-Attraction Friendship Leadership

I know that I'm respected. But when all the guys are friends, and you're a woman who isn't allowed to be friends with any of them, the same opportunities just won't be there. I show up for a pastors' conference, a rare opportunity for networking, and the only thing my peers ask is, "Where's your husband?" They feel uncomfortable around me; they feel like they shouldn't be talking to me because I'm a woman. They want me to go hang out with their wives (who are usually very nice, and I would love to spend time with them in different circumstances), but their wives aren't in vocational ministry. I am. And I'd like to build friendships with others in ministerial leadership. But my leaders, my supervisors, the people I rely on to help support me, seem like they honestly want nothing to do with me. (But they'll hang out with my husband.) And then I'm supposed to be surprised when all their "friends," the ones with whom they can play golf, or head to the movies, or grab a beer, those are the men asked to be keynote speakers or give presentations. And the introduction to those presentations almost always begins the same way:

Male leader on stage: "I'd like to welcome a very dear and personal friend of mine to be our speaker this evening. I've known him for years, and watched him grow through numerous life experiences." Another male leader climbs onto the stage.

And perhaps that man is better qualified than I am, and perhaps his presentation is better than anything I could have given. But I feel we'll never really know because I am denied that one thing that definitely separates him from me: he is allowed to be known through friendship and I am not.

One of the more challenging aspects of leading through friendship is this issue of gender and attraction. In my experience, this is cited as one of the most commonly expressed complications to arise in pursuit of friendship development. I believe there are two primary reasons to address this concern in a way that demonstrates inclusivity, health, and foresight:

## Denial of Friendship Equals Denial of Opportunity

Even in the most progressive institutions, where women in leadership are not only allowed but championed, there can still exist a disparate dissipation of opportunity. Human beings are relational; we gain trust through shared experience, common goals, and proven track records. As we share life together, we find out upon whom we can rely and to whom we can entrust more responsibility. In the absence of this "shared life," as can be the case for women breaking into predominately male-driven leadership platforms, there is a vacuum where there should be opportunity.

Think about the people you trust most, the ones you would call up in a crisis. Maybe it's the person you call because you know they can "get the job done." Now, think of how you *know* you can count on that person. Is it because of their resumé? Are they your go-to speaker/leader/manager because they look good on paper? Probably not. Most likely, you go to that person because over the course of your experience in leadership, they have shown themselves to be reliable and competent.

Yes, it is a two-way street—it is important for members of minority populations to take risks and grab opportunities as they arise. But what if the opportunity never formally arises? What if responsibilities are delegated in "backroom" conversations, instead of posted in public arenas? What if a position is privately appointed? In each of these scenarios, leaders determine who they will champion on the basis of personal relationship; often times, the first name that comes to mind is someone they would consider a friend.

Believe it or not, no one wants to be a "diversity" pick, selected merely because of their gender or race. Most often, the individual believes they are capable to fulfill the task at hand, and should be awarded opportunity on that fact alone. Not only can tokenism be demoralizing, but "diversity picks" can actually be harmful. If a woman is selected as the "token woman" at an event, yet she was only selected for that purpose (as opposed to being the right person for the task), then there is the risk that she will inaccurately represent the capabilities of women. If we only extend opportunities because we know we *should*, as opposed to joyfully raising up others from a place of relationship in response to their calling, skills, and experience, this may be an indication we could invest a little more time in diversified friendships.

In a focus group of women from a denomination that affirms women in all levels of leadership, Dr. Karen Tremper found that the opportunities available to women in the denomination did not always align with the vision.[1] She identified the greatest felt hindrances included:

- Opportunities were limited based on gender stereotypes. Friendship will keep us from limiting women to where we think they *should* be placed in a ministry context, and will instead allow them to inform us where they *actually belong*, based on their calling, skills, and experience. In the context of conferences and conventions, often women are expected to staff the "childcare" while the men attend the sessions. Without friendship, we can easily slip into stereotyping.

- Women do not have access to the "right networks." In a denomination that uses the appointment process for some opportunities, segregated networks (women only at women's events and men only at men's events) keep women from being "on the radar." Intentional friendship across lines will keep *everyone* on the radar.

- Men do not know how a woman "will fit" into a position of leadership. For some men, the culture of minority populations can be unfamiliar, and that unfamiliarity can lead to discomfort and avoidance. Friendship opens the door for other people groups and cultures to become familiar, easing the tension one might feel about appointing "the unknown," as friendship is all about knowing and being made known. This will also allow the space for others to retain their own culture and personality—for women, this means they will feel less pressure to adopt traditionally male interests. There will be freedom in friendship for true personalities to shine.

- The fear of sexual sin paralyzes relationships. I will write more on this subject later in the chapter, but for now, it needs to be mentioned that many women who participated in the study felt their opportunities were directly limited by the fears of men. From my experience, these fears are based on men's distrust of themselves and their own inability to have safe and healthy cross-attraction friendships. It's also worth

1. Tremper, *Credentialed Women in the Foursquare Church.*

noting that some women also felt suspicion from wives, the implied fear being that the women would steal the husbands. In all these scenarios, there is a lack of trust and love.

Although there are many factors contributing to the limited roles of women in leadership, and I do not claim that friendship is a cure-all, I think deliberate friendship can help overcome several obstacles we face going forward. This is not an argument against selecting leaders on the basis of personal experience—this is an important aspect of discernment—but rather, a plea to broaden the scope of friendship to include those who are usually relegated to the rank of "peer" or "coworker," instead of "friend."

## Broader Scope Calls for Deeper Reflection

As our churches, businesses, and ministries are growing more diverse in correlation to our society's expanding views regarding sex, gender, and sexual orientation, the questions and concerns regarding this facet of friendship will need to be more broadly anticipated and addressed. While previous generations may have "solved" this issue by merely forbidding the friendship between males and females, this "solution" will not suffice when we are leading members of the same sex or gender who also have a same-sex attraction or orientation. We need a more comprehensive approach to friendship as we venture into the future.

In the past few years, I've had the pleasure of welcoming a variety of people into our church body. I mentor, lead, and build friendships with those in my church, aware that the boundaries I establish with members of the opposite sex are now becoming relevant to those of my own sex.

As we lead people with same-sex attractions—regardless of our own views on the subject—we are called to do so in love. This means putting their needs in front of our own. So while it may be challenging work for some of us to re-evaluate some of these philosophies regarding the permissibility of friendship, it is quickly becoming an issue we cannot ignore if we hope to minister in love. Not only does the "just-avoid-all-members-of-the-opposite-sex" mentality dramatically decrease the opportunities available to others, but it will not stand as an effective boundary when leaders and followers alike might be drawn into a same-sex attraction. We need a thoughtful, biblical example to follow.

## How Does the Bible Address This Issue?

Before diving into the particulars of how to make this type of friendship possible, let us build a foundation from the Bible. Even within legalistic and patriarchal societies, there are still many examples of biblical cross-gender friendships. These serve as the guide we follow as we establish a clearer path to follow.

Beginning with the person of Jesus (our standard for Friendship Leadership), we encounter a leader who develops friendship with not only the male disciples, but also the female followers. In John 11, when Lazarus died, Jesus grieved alongside Mary and Martha, real tears and emotions coloring the sacred moment of friendship. In John 4, when he met the Samaritan woman, sitting all alone at a well, he spoke directly to her heart about subject matters taboo for the time. And when he rose from the dead, he spoke first to Mary Magdalene, inviting her into the knowledge of his deepest identity. Jesus, being the perfect embodiment of the love of God, was no doubt loved by the women in his life; perhaps some were even "in love" with him. Yet his perfect selfless love gave him the freedom to have healthy and holy friendships with these women.

In the Old Testament, we have stories like Deborah and Barak (Judg 4). The prophetess knew what God wanted to do in the life of Barak, but Barak required the support and presence of Deborah to walk into that call of battle. Theirs would resemble a modern-day workplace relationship built on respect for calling and skills. After their battle, Barak and Deborah sang together a song of victory. In the New Testament letters, Paul mentioned several women who had clearly earned his respect through shared experience including, but not limited to, Priscilla (Rom 16:3), Lois and Eunice (2 Tim 1:5), and Phoebe (Rom 16:1).

In fact, Paul gives us a method for cross-attraction friendship in his advice to Timothy: "Do not rebuke an older man harshly, but exhort him as if he were your father. Treat younger men as brothers, older women as mothers, and younger women as sisters, with absolute purity." (1 Tim 5:2). Instead of encouraging Timothy to abstain completely from interactions with women, Paul urges him to treat them as family. Here, one woman writes about how this passage helps her create healthy boundaries:

> I often think about the passage from First Timothy when I try to figure out my boundaries with friends who are male. I have a younger brother, and so if I am to treat all younger men as

brothers, then I just ask myself, "Would this be appropriate to do/say to Charlie (my brother)?" This leads me to some natural conclusions—I would talk to Charlie about my emotions, but I wouldn't talk to him about the details of my marriage. I would give him a friendly hug, but I wouldn't touch his knee (ew). This passage actually guides me clearly in what is appropriate behavior for my male friends. It allows me to extend the same friendship and care I have with Charlie to others in my life, while still providing a familiar framework within which I can relate.[2]

While it may seem naive to some to believe that in the midst of our oversexualized world, it is possible to relate to people we naturally find attractive in a pure and non-exploitive way, this is precisely what we must do. As the people of God are one body, one family, one Bride of Christ, let the biblical example of friendship empower us to reach across the lines that fear would have us create.

## Snapshots of Cross-Attraction Friendships in Christian History

Not limited to the time of the Bible, Christian history also gives us examples of cross-attraction friendships. I'm sure these relationships were not perfect (none are), but they demonstrate to us that the love and respect we find in God can be shared in a healthy way with those God brings into our lives. Here are just two snapshots:

### William Penn and Margaret Fell

Although many may be familiar with the name of George Fox, father of Quakerism, and William Penn, founder of the colony of Pennsylvania, fewer may be familiar with Fox's wife, Margaret Fell, and the friendship shared by all three.[3] Fell is often considered the matriarch of Quakerism. She offered her home for meetings, often preaching and risking her land and position for her beliefs. She even served four years in prison when the government cracked down on the Quaker movements. During this time, she met and married her second husband, George Fox (her first husband had passed away). It was unusual for a woman to surpass so many barriers,

2. First person account from the author, Rachel McMurray-Branscombe.

3. Kunze, "Religious Authority and Social Status," 170–86.

both as a leader within her religious organization and as a woman who married beneath her social station. This break from traditional views of women allowed her to devote her life to ministry, alongside her husband.

When Fell and Fox decided to marry, a new aristocratic convert to Quakerism named William Penn attended their wedding. As a new Quaker, he fell under their guidance (by this point, they had both risen to a place of leadership within the organization). Penn pulled some strings to have Fox released from jail when he was imprisoned for preaching, aided in printing of Fox's books, and supported the couple through a rebellion in the Society.

When Penn married his wife, Gulielma Penn, the two couples developed a strong bond. Though the husbands were of different social standing, there existed a close friendship between them. And both wives were often in correspondence, sending letters and gifts, encouraging each other through the trials of ministry and life.

Fell, however, had inherited land from her first husband's death, making her a member of the gentry (as the land was in her name, Fox was not considered gentry). For this reason, an understanding developed between William Penn (also gentry) and Margaret Fell over their years of ministry— they both shared in this struggle of great risk and sacrifice to engage in their ministerial calling. In fact, Fell was described as being an "adopted mother" to the Penns, offering them affection as a friend and counsel as a leader.

Over the years, historians like Bonnelyn Young Kunze have been able to piece together epistolary insight into this friendship between Margaret Fell and William Penn. In leadership, Penn reported to Fell, specifically regarding his missionary ventures. In friendship, Penn would write: "Truly sweet and precious is the holy fellowship that our dear Lord has given us together in his own pure eternal spirit . . ."[4] Though Fell maintained a position as a leader in Penn's life, their correspondence showed a deep respect and affection.

These two families were so close that Fox and Fell's children would travel with Penn on his missionary voyages. And when George Fox passed away, it was William Penn who wrote Margaret Fell of the news. Of their friendship, Kunze notes, "Penn achieved in his steady thirty-year friendship with Fell a depth, warmth, and closeness to her that suggests natural congeniality and intimacy felt between friends of the same social milieu."[5]

4. Kunze, "Religious Authority and Social Status," 175.

5. Kunze, "Religious Authority and Social Status," 185.

Within this story of close friendship, we still can find the balance of freedom and boundaries. As co-laborers in ministry, Fell and Penn were able to engage in friendship with a familial quality. However, there was nothing secretive about the friendship—both couples openly encouraged each other, allowing respectful friendship to grow through time, and shared experience. Though I've chosen to focus on this one specific friendship, both Fell and Penn displayed this value of Friendship Leadership with countless members of the Society of Friends, irrespective of class or gender.

## C.S. Lewis and Arthur Greeves

As a writer, I've always loved the image of the Inklings: a group of academics from Oxford, sitting in the back room of a cozy pub, reading aloud excerpts from their current projects, with captivating character names like Gandalf, Aslan, and Father Brown. As famous as C.S. Lewis would become through his writings, he is almost equally known for the friendships he kept with visionaries like J.R.R. Tolkien, G.K. Chesterton, and George MacDonald. As the stories reveal, Lewis made a lifelong habit of investing in friendship. True, there were those like him—male academics and authors (like those found in the Inklings). But there were others, too: people from a different background, gender, or sexual orientation than his. One such person was Arthur Greeves.

Lewis met Greeves when they were both sixteen years old.[6] Greeves, a neighbor in Belfast, had become sick and asked Lewis to visit him at his home. Sitting there on a nightstand by the sickbed was a book about Norse mythology, and that was all that was needed to begin a friendship that would span thirty years of life. Though their lives took very different paths, with Lewis setting out on a hedonistic journey (contrary to Greeves' Christian lifestyle), they remained quite close through letter writing. They shared their youthful follies, the daily minutia, and the big life questions together.

After several years, and through the influence of many friends, Lewis would embark on his own relationship with Jesus Christ, a fact he first revealed to his childhood friend. Lewis would describe Greeves as "after my brother, my oldest and most intimate friend."[7] This intimacy didn't lessen even as Greeves revealed his same-sex attractions.[8] Though Lewis, himself,

6. Lewis, *They Stand Together*.

7. "C.S. Lewis," para. 12.

8. Hill, "C.S. Lewis' Deep Friendship With Arthur Greeves."

didn't believe acting on same-sex attraction was morally acceptable, the conviction didn't lessen their connection as friends in any discernible way. Over the course of close to 300 letters sent by Lewis to Greeves,[9] a habit they maintained all the way up to Lewis' death, Lewis never shied away from a deep and intimate friendship with Greeves. Having meaningful friendships, even where same-sex attraction exists, is possible, and as the friendship of Lewis and Greeves demonstrates, it can be life-giving.

## But What About Boundaries?

That's the big question you're probably all asking right now. And you are right to ask this. We are sadly too familiar with stories of ministries lost to sexual or emotional sin. This should not lead us to complete abstention from friendship, but rather a necessary conversation about boundaries. *All* relationships have boundaries. Every healthy relationship, whether it's with family members, friends, followers, coworkers, has clear boundaries. These boundaries are not meant to hinder, but to give freedom in our expression of care. I'm sure our exact boundaries will differ on this subject, but for cross-attraction Friendship Leadership, I find these to be my non-negotiable boundaries:

- Refrain from sexualized or sexually-related conversations. Though we live in a Christian culture that is trying to reclaim an open conversation about Godly sexuality, this is not an excuse to engage in conversation that does not build "others up, according to their needs, that it may benefit those who listen" (Eph 4:29).

- Refrain from discussions around topics of intimacy with spouse or significant other, unless that person is present. Limit accountability relationships to individuals with whom attraction (on your side and/ or theirs) is not a temptation.

- Refrain from conversations that begin to foster an emotional intimacy without the inclusion of one's spouse or significant other. As we begin to form friendships, we will form emotional connections. This isn't necessarily a bad thing, but it quickly becomes dangerous if it excludes a spouse (or trusted accountability partner for a single person). I may have a moving conversation with a coworker about an

9. "C.S. Lewis," para. 13.

emotionally-challenging situation in ministry—but not only do I talk with my wife about the situation, I tell her about the conversation with the coworker. Because we are one, she is included in all my emotional connections.

• Refrain from developing a friendship of unhealthy dependency. If I feel that a cross-attraction friend is being drawn into the relationship with me in order to fulfill their emotional vulnerability or needs, I have learned to back away while directing them towards other relationships where that need could be met in a healthy and productive way. As leaders we have a responsibility to be "safe" as we care for people who are working through their own brokenness and neediness.

Some boundaries are personal and negotiable based on the person and the circumstance. Though I share my boundaries with you, please do not use them as a license to dismiss the conviction of the Holy Spirit in your life regarding your boundaries. This process of discerning non-negotiable boundaries should include your spouse and an accountability partner. They should be communicated to the people who know and love you. If you do not work with your spouse, when possible, have a coworker hold you accountable, as they interact with you throughout the day. These boundaries may need to be modified based on your natural weaknesses and proclivities.

Beyond the non-negotiables, however, there are boundaries of what I would consider "to each their own." For example, as a running enthusiast, I have had a lot of running friends and teammates who were women, but these friendships have never been private. Friendship was experienced within a larger accountable community. I also work alongside women, so I have boundaries that allow for meaningful interactions while staying accountable and professional. I engage in social media interaction that is non-sexual and not feeding emotional needs that should be met by my wife, but I also stick to mediums that allow for ongoing accountability (which is why I avoid social media apps with "disappearing" message systems). These types of boundaries have been established in conversations with my wife, and she has her own boundaries based on her convictions, ministry, and personality. They are unique to us, communicated clearly, and spirit-inspired, all with the goal of engaging everyone in the freedom found in love.

Cross-attractional friendship needs to come from a place of health, however, and some people are too broken to express love without it devolving into something self-serving. If this is your honest assessment of yourself, and you are unable to maintain these types of friendships right now, there is absolutely no shame in that admission. If you feel that a friendship may be getting drawn in too close, you have to pull away (while remaining friends), without causing them to stumble emotionally. I would ask, however, that you consider establishing your boundaries in a way that does not force the people in your life to pay the price for your personal issues. For example, I have seen leaders fire or remove a coworker from leadership due to their attraction to that person (a form of sexual harassment)—this is an example of a very unloving way to establish boundaries.

Ultimately, we need to be able to *love* people, regardless of sex or basic attraction. We just have to share a healthy love that celebrates people; their personality, beauty, and God-given uniqueness. Jesus figured this out and I think some people can do this as well. Don't operate out of fear. Our choices should be motivated by conscientious wisdom.

## Creative Opportunities:

I wouldn't be much help to you if I only wrote about what *not* to do, without giving you some ideas of what you can do. There are probably many more ideas to be added to this list, but for now, I leave you with these creative possibilities:

- Do not engage in gender discrimination because of your cross at-tractional realities. Your position of leadership gives a framework for a natural progression of workplace relationships. You have topics to discuss (challenges, questions, victories) and a reason for discussing them. As you lead, think through the logistics: What do you need to do to be safe and accountable? I know we may feel tempted at times to choose relationships that are easiest to accomplish, but don't let logis-tics keep you from your role as leader.

- Invest in friendships as couples. My wife and I have many "couple friends," husbands and wives with whom we take time together to in-vest in friendship. We love to travel, eat good food, go to sports games, play board games, and enjoy life together. While the four of us spend time together, I am able to invest in my friendship with both the hus-band and the wife, as is Heidi. This provides a safe context to get to know people as I am creating friendship alongside my wife.

- Love, but do it in a *healthy* way with that person's best interest in mind. All friendship should be an extension of what God offers us, a love that meets us where we are. The truth is that friendship built in *agapé* love precludes any hurtful action. The more I truly become friends with someone, the less likely I am to do anything or allow anything that could hurt someone or their family. God's love leaves no room for selfish action. This is why it is imperative that all friendships be founded on that perfect, selfless love.

Within my life, however, is the knowledge that while I love everyone, I love my wife in a special way. I've had many friends that were female; interns, mentorees, and athletes I've coached. I love them deeply as people. I just have a compartment of my love that is reserved exclusively for Heidi. Any love I have for friends should not compare to this special love I share with my wife. Healthy friendships build up the things that are important to each friend: their marriages, families, ministries, etc.

As we follow the example of Jesus in his demonstration of Friendship Leadership, we must acknowledge that his commitment to the practice wasn't limited to certain races, credos, or genders. It was offered to everyone he encountered, spurred on by his eternal understanding of relationship and selfless love. The love in our leadership should build others up, not build up walls that prevent others' growth or realization of potential.

# 11

## The Introverted Leader Friend

As I've been presenting the concept of this book to friends and co-workers, several people have indicated an interest in how this concept of Friendship Leadership is applied to the leadership of an introvert. If you happen to be an extrovert, you may want to go ahead and skip ahead to chapter 12. But if you prefer a small number of friends, read on.

As an introvert myself, I can attest to the power and possibility of friendship within my own leadership personality. Sometimes, the friendship has come easily; other times, it has required a bit of work. My life and ministry have demonstrated to me that Friendship Leadership for introverts is attainable, and this section will demonstrate that it's possible not *in spite of* the introverted personality, but in many ways, *because* of it.

### What Does It Mean To Be an Introvert?

Though many definitions of "introverted and extroverted" personalities have surfaced over the years, these terms were first popularized by Swiss psychiatrist and psychoanalyst, Carl Jung. Susan Cain, author of *Quiet: The Power of Introverts in a World that Can't Stop Talking*, summed up the Jungian understanding of these personalities: "Introverts are drawn to the inner world of thought and feeling," while "extroverts to the external life of people and activities. Introverts focus on the meaning they make of the events swirling around them; extroverts plunge into the events themselves. Introverts recharge their batteries by being alone; extroverts need to recharge when they don't socialize enough."[1] Another way to consider this is

1. Cain, *Quiet*, 10.

to monitor your energy level throughout the day; as you are surrounded by people, or spend time alone, how do your emotions and thoughts fluctuate? When do you "need a break from people," or when do you experience "cabin fever"? These answers can help direct your own understanding of your personality.

Beyond Jung, Jerome Kagan, developmental psychologist, conducted a study of individuals with a high or low reactivity to external stimuli, like noise, meeting strangers, and seeing colors. There was a correlation between high-reactivity and introversion. Kagan's study describes more than just personality; it shows us human temperament, or "inborn, biologically based behavioral and emotional patterns,"[2] as opposed to what is fostered within us through life experience. This means that an introvert could be born highly reactive to the external world, and no amount of conditioning can completely alter that level of reactivity.

This idea that introversion relates to an aversion for novel external stimulation could indicate that an individual who dislikes large, loud parties *isn't* anti-social—they just don't like crowded, rowdy environments. Cain says that, "introversion is a preference for environments that are not overstimulating."[3] So for some people, their hesitation in social environments isn't relational, but contextual.

In one example of how personality affects stimulation preference, introverts and extroverts were both given a word puzzle to solve, and then asked to dial in the optimum level of background music. On average, the introverts selected a lower level of volume (55 decibels) compared to the extroverts (72 decibels), demonstrating that for introverts, a little stimulation goes a long way.

Finally, in the description of introverts, it's important to note that it does *not* necessarily mean shy, misanthropic, or hermit-like. Though some cases of introversion may take on these characteristics or roles, they are not an integral part of this personality type.

As you've been reading this description of introversion, hopefully you have a rough understanding of where you fall on the introversion-extroversion spectrum. I won't dive into that here in this book, but if you are unfamiliar with your own personality type, I encourage you to check out one of the many of personality tests available to you in print or online.

2. Cain, *Quiet,* 100.

3. Cain, *Quiet,* 12.

Speaking personally, I am an introvert (which should come as a shock to no one who knows me). As an introvert, most of my friends are aware of my morning ritual: a long, solitary run (my only company: a Jack Russell terrier, who doesn't require much conversation), followed by an hour or so of quiet reflective prayer, study, and reading. This prepares me for my day. In my free time, I have always preferred individual sports and activities. Surfing, solo mountain climbing, and fishing alone leave me recharged. And if you've been in my house in the later hours of the evening, you know it is not uncommon for me to excuse myself from company and head to bed, leaving my guests and my wife to talk until the early hours of the morning, if they so choose. True, some of this is because I'm biologically wired as a "morning person," but I find these boundaries help create space in my life for "restorative niches," something I'll address further in this section.[4]

This chapter is based on generalized descriptions of introversion. Of course, every individual person differs from the majority in some way. Also, this is not in praise or criticism of one personality over the other. My focus on introversion is due to the common belief that introverts aren't as "friendly" as extroverts (a perception I believe we should challenge). But I firmly believe this: as one body and one team, we need each other, introverts and extroverts alike.

## Positive Social Abilities for Introverts:

While occasionally a situation may call for you to tap into an extroverted frame of mind, there are positive qualities embedded within the introverted personality that present unique abilities applicable to Friendship Leadership. This chapter isn't about training you to be different than you are, but rather, it is about how to harness your strengths within friendship. You can use Friendship Leadership *because* of your personality, rather than in spite of it, as some would have you believe. So if you've ever worried you wouldn't be able to participate well in friendship because you're an introvert, just enjoy this list:

4. Cain, *Quiet,* 218.

## Introverted Social Ability #1: Focus

Introverts tend to focus on one thing at a time, harnessing their mental faculties into a laser-like focus. This can be channeled into interests like biology or music; it can also be useful for building empathy and investing in a personal relationship. As introverted leaders, we focus on what matters to us—our relationships.

I have a friend, John, who admits that, as an introvert, he sometimes has a hard time focusing on small talk and "shallower" conversation. Instead of leaving the conversation or shutting down, however, he decided a few years ago that he would tap into his introversion for the good of the conversation. As he engages in these types of conversations, he intentionally fans the flame of curiosity within himself, focusing on certain details about the other person's life. Suddenly, small talk isn't tedious; it's helping him discover vital information about who that person really is. His wife even laughs at him sometimes, as she claims she can tell when he "flips the switch" in his brain, turning on his curiosity and his love of discovery. Because of that focus, he actually walks away from seemingly unimportant conversations with a wealth of knowledge about people and a deeper empathy because he understands them a little more.

## Introverted Social Ability #2: Thoughtful Speech

Though the average introvert doesn't exactly bubble over with an enthusiastic effluence of conversation, it doesn't mean their words are worth anything less. Not only do introverts often listen more, they think before they speak, which gives them space to be intentional about encouragement and support. Introverts may say less than they want to, but they also don't have to apologize as much as they would need to if they talked without thinking.

## Introverted Social Ability #3: Emotional Intelligence

Studies have shown that introverted children, when raised in a nurturing supporting environment, can be *more* successful in social settings than their extroverted counterparts, specifically because they take the time to observe the social setting first.[5] I'll admit that being an introvert—and having to work at stretching my comfort zone—has given me numerous opportuni-

5. Cain, *Quiet*, 111.

ties for developing my social awareness and relationship management. For introverts, who carefully monitor the social dynamics before deciding to join in, that time of observation can reveal any number of small emotional nuances taking place and inform future engagement. If you are an extrovert working with an introvert, I would encourage you to heed their observations—it's one of their strengths.

## Introverted Social Ability #4: Genuineness

"I work with another leader. She is, well, she's charming, funny and fun. She's the kind of person everyone wants to be around. When you're with her, you're always laughing and the time just seems to fly by! Everyone wants to be where she is, and when you leave her, you feel certain that you're the best of friends." Anne was describing an extroverted friend. "The truth is, *everyone* feels that way. And it can be a little disappointing when you realize that's just how she makes people feel. There's nothing wrong with it; you just may not be the best friends you thought you were." Anne, the introvert, concluded: "Yeah, people don't have that problem with me."

Especially within Friendship Leadership, it is a strength for people to be able to read you correctly. I would say that sometimes, the absence of overt gregariousness can be a strength. For Anne's friend, putting other people at ease and making them feel special are some of her strengths. But for Anne, it's precisely *because* she takes her time developing the warmth of friendship that when someone feels it, they know it's a special bond and absolutely legitimate (perhaps even more than they know). As long as true and kind friendship is being pursued, both the introverted and extroverted personality types have something unique to offer.

## Tips for Introverted Friendship Leadership

Building on the strengths of introverts, how can we develop a life of Friendship Leadership? What tools are at our disposal? What boundaries do we need to set up? Although I'm sure you can think up some of your own answers to these questions, here are a few thoughts from my own experience as an introverted leader friend:

## Tips on Building Friendships:

- *Prioritize.* Despite what some might think, extroverts can't befriend everyone. If you're like me, you can feel guilty at times, because you feel as though you're never doing "enough," and you're convinced that there's some extrovert who is somehow magically doing "enough." This isn't true. Introverts and extroverts both feel like there's more that can be done do to invest in relationships. So, as an introvert, spend a good percentage of your time investing in your particular strength: focus on deep, instead of wide. For example, when you go to a dinner party, don't allow yourself to be consumed with regret that you can't float effervescently from crowd to crowd, making pleasant small talk with every person. As a leader, you may need to greet everyone with a friendly disposition, but also give yourself permission to find one person with whom you'd like to develop more friendship, and focus on that one person (OK, maybe two, if you're feeling extra outgoing).

- *Take advantage of "passive" forms of communication,* which have been found useful in groups of introverts. Sure, face-to-face is often the best for those "big" conversations, but if you feel writing emails, letters, or postcards eases some of the anxiety, use these as tools to strengthen your communication. I have an introverted coworker who prefers to write out a sort of "script" for important conversations, bringing it with her into meetings; she may even send this script in an email ahead of the face-to-face discussion, so both parties can feel prepped before they walk into the conversation. As an introvert, she prefers taking the time to think through what she' would like to communicate, and often feels more successful at the end of such conversations.

- *In a workplace environment, consider the online tools at your disposal* (for meetings, file sharing, and brainstorming). If you are an introvert without a private space at work, consider asking for a few outside-the-office hours to spend at either a quiet coffee shop or at home, where you can still communicate with coworkers, but from a more restoring place. Online classrooms have also revolutionized the way we make passive communication more commonplace, allowing introverts to study and collaborate from a location less anxiety-inducing as a lecture hall of 500 students. I would caution, however, to not hide completely online, as we develop more trust in the relationship through face-to-face interactions than we do in pure online interactions. Passive communication is certainly a tool that works well with the introvert's personality, but a bit of stretching is also important.

- *Foster a keen curiosity about people.* As with the story of John, many introverts report high levels of curiosity about the world around them. Instead of trying to repress the cerebral part of your personality, direct it so that it lines up with what you care about: people. This is why our friendships must have pure motivation; if we don't genuinely care about people, it will be hard to bring our active brains in line with our heart. But when they interact harmoniously and we respond with curiosity to the people we love, it's a beautiful thing.

- *Sometimes, the answer is taking a little* more *initiative, not less.* Says one introverted friend of mine, "I host parties at my house precisely *because* I'm an introvert. Since the event is at my house, I know what and who to expect. The surroundings are comfortable. And if I ever get overwhelmed, I can just disappear into my room for a couple minutes, or suddenly become 'occupied' with my hosting duties." Instead of withdrawing from the idea of Friendship Leadership, try to take initiative to build friendships that take into consideration your comfort levels. Introverts don't need to play the role of social victim: they are a living organic component to how friendships exist and evolve. I have grown more social with time. This has been a result of overcoming my own fears and insecurities while trying to follow the example of Jesus and the mandate to love.

- *Build friendship around deep interests.* It's a common stereotype of the introvert that they loathe small talk. I would have to say that I'm not too fond of it, myself. Since you know you prefer to talk about certain subjects on a deep level, lean in to that. Discover friends who share similar interests, and unapologetically pursue them together. Just as C.S. Lewis and Arthur Greeves became friends based on a common love for Norse mythology, you may discover your own lifelong friends by accepting, not denying, your deep interests.

- *Appreciate the extroverts in your life.* Studies show that introverts and extroverts actually experience a degree of relief when communicating with each other, as they intuitively know the other personality can add something to their life that is missing.[6] While we may be initially

6. Cain, *Quiet,* 239.

drawn to people like us, please don't apply Friendship Leadership only to those who share your same personality type. As I mentioned before, we need each other. Take the time and effort to cultivate a friendship with people different than you.

## Tips for "Restorative Niches":

- *Find a balance of stretching your personality and "restorative niches,"*[7] a term developed by Professor Brian Little, psychology lecturer at Harvard University, to describe "the place you go when you want to return to your true self."[8] For me, one example of a restorative niche is the time I take between our two Sunday morning services. Sharing a sermon can be a vulnerable experience, and absorbing the attention of hundreds of people at a time can be emotional work. So I have developed a habit of slipping away for fifteen minutes, closing my office door, and enjoying a cup of coffee before the second service begins. Sometimes, I sit all alone, praying and resting. Other times, my wife is there, and I enjoy sharing a quiet moment with her before returning to the crowds. An introverted leader and friend needs to intentionally build in restorative niches.

- *Pay attention to your body, mind, and heart*—they could be giving you signals about your boundaries. One of my introverted pastor friends shared that he began to experience anxiety attacks a couple years ago. His heart would start to race and he would feel sick to his stomach. Concerned, he visited his doctor, who had him wear a heart monitor for a couple weeks. When the results came in from the test, he noticed a particular pattern: though his heart rate fluctuated every day, there were a couple hours every week when his heart would rise to 150 BPM and sit there for hours. Can you guess when that was? If you guessed Sunday mornings, you would be correct. Though he enjoyed his ministerial position and the people in his church, he took this as a sign that perhaps he needed to restructure how he approached his stimulation levels on Sunday mornings.

---

7. Cain, *Quiet,* 218.

8. Cain, *Quiet,* 200.

- If Friendship Leadership is a priority, *you may need to rethink some of your lesser priorities.* Are there times in your day when you are needlessly overexposing yourself to stimulation (for example, working in a loud coffee shop instead of the quiet of your home)? Are there times when you could make a small change that would reframe the experience so it revitalizes you (closing your office door for twenty minutes)? Do you need to attend *everything*? As senior pastor, I am invited to every activity/event/ministry within my church, as well as countless community projects. I cannot participate in everything, so I prioritize—not based on the importance of the event, but on the investments in relationships I feel are necessary. Friendship is a high priority in my leadership, so some evenings, my wife and I will choose to have a couple from our church over for dinner, rather than head out to the big fundraising gala. This corresponds with my introversion, and reaffirms my commitment to deep friendship.

- Finally, *we can find confidence in the knowledge that God knows* we need this time of rest and restoration. It's why he set the example for us of a sabbath time. Whether you are introverted or extroverted, plan some regular ongoing time to dedicate to revitalization, inviting the Holy Spirit into the experience with you. I also encourage leaders to work a sabbatical into their long-term goals. My wife and I made time this last year for our first sabbatical in twenty-five years of ministry. It wasn't prompted by burnout or negativity, but rather a desire to prioritize a time of deliberate self- and couple-investment. It made us better friends and better leaders.

## Tips on Self-Acceptance:

- *Don't let peer pressure push you to be someone you're not.* Just because a coworker demonstrates Friendship Leadership by inviting a different person over to their house every single evening, that doesn't mean you're a failure at Friendship Leadership just because you prefer to reserve your evenings for rest and rebuilding. Trying to be like someone else, trying to be someone other than who you are, will lead to burnout. We can be inspired by other leaders, but we cannot *be* them. Instead, creatively consider how you can invest in the qualities of friendship—initiative, time, loyalty and commitment, priority, communication, encouragement, respect, intimacy—in a way that reflects who *you* are. (Notice: none of those qualities are reserved only for the extroverted.)

- *Challenge how you interpret "leadership."* Going back to the original definition of leadership in this book as "the influence of others towards a greater love of God and people," leadership can take many different forms, from a gregarious upfront spokesperson, to a quiet influencer working behind the scenes, connecting with one person at a time. Studies also show that introverts are better leaders when it comes to teams of "initiative-takers," while extroverts are better leaders on teams where members are more passive.[9] Your environment, your team, and your goals may just be perfectly suited for an introverted leader and friend!

- As you do stretch the outer limits of your exposure to social situations and external stimulation, *make sure it's in the service of something or someone you truly care about.* Most personality experts believe that we can "borrow" from other personalities from time to time, but we are most successful with this when our motives are genuine and authentic to who we are. This also resolves the worry that such "borrowing" from extroverts is disingenuous. If the love is real, and the care genuine, then the expression is truthful. Just remember that when we talk about "borrowing" some extroverted personality traits, we're talking about short-term behavior modifications, not long-term self-denial, or self-rejection.

- Finally, *this isn't about pretending to be an extrovert.* It's about being an introverted friend and leader. Too long acting out of character can negatively affect your perception, your health, your emotions, your anxiety levels, your relationships, and well, you get the idea. While there are always times to stretch and grow in weak areas, try to be a leader friend who develops relationships out of authentically being known.

9. Cain, *Quiet*, 57.

## How to Lead When Your Friends Are Introverts

Florence was an introvert in an extrovert's world. Early in her leadership, she had received feedback that her social engagement was, at times, "intimidating and strong." For this reason, she had carefully cultivated a cheerier persona, specifically designed to help others see her as "friendly and approachable." As a manager in charge of several teams of people, she used this personality shift to put people at ease, and it worked . . . most of the time. One time, however, Florence gained a new team member who didn't seem to jell with her friendly outgoing persona. *It must be that I'm not friendly enough. I'll try harder,* she thought. She offered smiles, warmth, and a sunny disposition to her employee, only to feel the distance between them grow larger. Finally, after the entire business participated in personality assessments did she discover the problem: they were both introverts.

Florence realized she had been approaching the situation from the wrong direction. She decided to interact with and engage the team member as she *wished other people would engage her.* She dropped the false pleasantness, the small talk, and the warm laughter. She was direct—blunt, even!—no longer worried she would seem "intimidating." From the outside, one could even think their exchanges were cold, but as a result of this change, she began immediately to bond with the employee. They found that they were actually operating on the same wavelength. I'm happy to report that theirs evolved into an ongoing relationship of Friendship Leadership.

As you lead introverted friends, whether you are an introvert or extrovert yourself, I would encourage you to keep these helpful tips in mind:

- *Don't force them.* No one likes to be forced in a relationship, but an introverted friend could experience intense anxiety. As a leader, don't push friends to become highly involved in *everything* you are doing. (In a church setting, that would look like attending every prayer session, Bible study, small group, choir practice, and MOPS gathering, just because you're their senior pastor and friend.) Let them pick and choose what works for them and their priorities. For leaders in the Christian context, consider reading *Introverts in the Church: Finding Our Place in an Extroverted Culture.* Create space in the relationship for the introverted friend to approach in a manner that works with their personality.

- *Respect their time, privacy, and space.* In this day and age, it's hard enough to set boundaries, so let's cheer on our friends when they do.

Communicate through issues about time, privacy, and space, being honest about expectations. And when they express boundaries, avoid creating an atmosphere of guilt. As you lead, think: gentle caregiver, not drill sergeant.

- *Acknowledge what spending time with you really means to them*—it's an act of sacrifice and love. For some, time investment costs very little from an emotional or mental perspective (in fact, for some, it actually pours into them); for these people, it may be hard to appreciate what it costs an introvert. As someone who practices Friendship Leadership, I try to stay aware of how my friends under my ministry show up for events and opportunities, demonstrating appreciation when I can.

- *Sometimes, just skip over what they see as unnecessary social mores.* It presents them with more emotional work and complicates the communication. Instead, if you feel like you can address something with one word instead of two—try it.

- *Pay attention to context.* Remember: it's not always about people, but overstimulation. So meet the introverts under your leadership somewhere they're comfortable (perhaps a quiet office or coffee shop, instead of a big ministry mixer). And outside the office, they may not want to join you for large group parties, but they'd love to go on a walk with you.

- *Let them focus on you, ask questions, and dig a little deeper.* This is a form of relational investment. And try it out yourself—not only will you discover something new about your introverted friend, but they feel your care through your interest.

- *Don't take their overstimulation personally.* By integrating friendship into our leadership, it means we are more emotionally vulnerable and susceptible to hurt. For that reason, we may be extra-sensitive, searching for the deeper dangers in friendship. But when an introverted friend you lead pulls away, it doesn't necessarily mean there's a problem in the relationship; it could just mean they are retreating to a restorative niche. Give them time, and then check back in.

As leaders who influence through friendship, let's build up the strengths of others, utilizing our best traits for the flourishing of relationships. This leadership model is not limited to certain personalities, but is available to every person in their own unique way.

# 12

## Conclusion

ALTHOUGH I LIVED IN Bend for a year, Coos Bay, Oregon, is my hometown. It is a former logging and fishing town with a lost identity that boasts some breathtaking coastline. Early in ministry I had the opportunity to take my young family there to serve as a youth pastor at a small church. While there I discovered the joy of surfing. The Oregon waters were cold and "sharky," but they also were a constant beckoning adventure just waiting to happen.

Trevor was a senior in high school and felt the "call" to vocational ministry. He also loved the ocean. We began unskilled weekly forays into the swells where we survived near-drowning and hypothermic experiences, punctuated by laughter and pure adrenaline. Learning to surf is extremely difficult. Experienced surfers stay away from beginners for good reason. On one occasion, I was riding a wave straight towards another surfer who was paddling out. I wanted to avoid a collision, so I jumped off my board. Instead of "running him over" I sent my board straight at his terrified face. He came out of the water with a bloody nose and some expletives that seemed fitting for the moment. I felt terrible for him and was thankful he did not return the favor by physically assaulting me. These shared experiences deepened a bond of friendship with Trevor that was stronger than the beatings that we took.

Upon graduation, Trevor chose to pursue vocational ministry—he was going to be a pastor. I knew that our friendship contributed more to the pursuit of his "calling" than the sermons I had preached at him as a youth pastor. Surfing, paintball, camps, and road trips had created a foundation of friendship that multiplied the mutual influence that we had on each other. At the time, I had no idea how far that influence would go.

After graduating from Bible college, Trevor became a youth pastor in Des Moines, Washington, where he began pouring himself into his students. Following a model of ministry that was highly relational, Trevor did far more than teach curriculum. He made friendship a cornerstone in his leadership.

There was a student in Trevor's youth group there in Des Moines who, like Trevor, felt a call to vocational ministry. His name was Sean.

Fast forward to fifteen years later. Sean followed a pathway into vocational ministry and became the junior high youth pastor at the church where I was serving. My son, Levi, was now in his youth group. I appreciated the fact that Sean organized "movie marathons" with the kids. On one occasion, they watch all the *Rocky* movies while doing physical competitions that mimic Rocky's training (aside from boxing each other). Another favorite activity was an elaborate form of Hide and Seek called "Fugitive," resulting in a visit from the police (they were being so stealthy the neighbors became suspicious). They attended camps and retreats, and went on mission trips—sealing the bond of friendship between leader and follower.

Levi helped lead music at summer camps that were directed by Sean and friendship gave them a strong foundation to work together. Levi said, "We sometimes disagreed on what songs to do, but because of the depth of our friendship, we could have honest dialogue. Without friendship, people are less open and honest with each other while working together and that doesn't improve creativity or effectiveness." Levi ended up moving to Uganda for six months following graduation. When he returned to the U.S. and needed a place to live, Sean and his wife, April, were there for him while he found a job and got back on his feet.

My investment in Friendship Leadership had come full circle, blessing my own son fifteen years after I invested in one of my junior high students. In rapid succession I could see the domino effect of Friendship Leadership resulting in transformed lives and relationships that are rich, eternal, and intergenerational.

It's like something from the Bible, a list of "begets" demonstrating the faithfulness of God to move in every generation and multiply his good works.

Jerry was a friend to me.

I was a friend to Trevor.

Trevor was a friend to Sean.

And Sean was a friend to my own son, Levi.

I know that Levi will continue on this path of Friendship Leadership, not because he follows my example, but because his own life was transformed by the moving power of this kind of influence.

This is just one personal example of the power of Friendship Leadership. I have seen it work in nearly every leadership context, resulting in greater influence. It is rooted in a biblical theology and the model of Jesus. It is built upon the supreme ethic to "love your neighbor as yourself."

## The Dream

I dream of the day when leaders will fearlessly invest their hearts and their lives into their followers, creating a culture where love and acceptance are palpable. Through Friendship Leadership, creativity and passion will flourish in organizations of all hierarchical structures. The workplace will be a place where it is a joy to interact with one's friends while pursuing a common mission. Managers and subordinates will have an environment that fosters mentoring in an accelerated fashion. Leaders will no longer be kept isolated and out of touch due to fear-based barriers. Instead, they will be free to know the dreams of people throughout the organizational structure.

Work will no longer be a barrier to friendship. By giving it a place to grow in professional environments, the quality of people's lives will be enhanced.

## The Appeal

Let's get started. Why wait another day? Let it be something you champion. Let friendship be something you foster and encourage in others. Let Friendship Leadership form the way you lead, the activities you plan, the way you approach leaders, subordinates, stakeholders, and customers. Embrace this with joy and sincerity. Having counted the cost, the rewards far outweigh the risks.

# Discussion Questions

## Part I: Discovering Friendship Leadership

### Chapter 1: The Story of a Friend

- Is "friendship with God" something you long for?

  - Why or why not?

- Does it diminish or enhance your view God's omnipotence and sovereignty?

### Chapter 2: The Christian Legacy of Friendship Leadership

- Have you ever felt God's invitation of friendship extended to you? How have you experienced this friendship in your life? Do you feel the Creator Friend walking alongside you? Do you harbor any doubts about God wanting to lead you through friendship?

- As you look back into your past, think about the religious leaders you've experienced. What kind of leadership did they model to you? How did their example of leadership shape the way you lead now? Were there aspects of relationship you wish you had received from them that you didn't?

- As you consider your current relationships of leadership, how well do you exemplify the leadership of Jesus? Do you "make things known" to them? Who in your sphere of influence has experienced pain, rejection, joy, and uncertainty alongside you?

# Part II: Practicing Friendship Leadership

## Chapter 3: Friendship Leadership Defined

- Which of the qualities of friendship do you appreciate the most from others?
- Which of the qualities of friendship do you find the most difficult to give to others?
- Revisit the definitions of leadership and friendship. What is your immediate reaction to these definitions? (Hope? Hesitation? Resistance? Excitement?) Why?

## Chapter 4: The Benefits of Friendship Leadership

- Of the benefits of Friendship Leadership, which would contribute the most to your life right now?
- When friendship is not valued, certain dangers exist. Which ones are you facing in your organization?

## Chapter 5: Qualities in Friendship Leadership

- Which of the qualities of friendship come most naturally to you? Where does your personality intersect the qualities of a good friend?
- Which of the qualities of friendship are hardest for you to practice? What are some ways you can intentionally work to strengthen this area?

## Chapter 6: People in Friendship Leadership

- Which is flourishing in your life right now: friendship with God, friendship with self, or friendship with others? How have you invested in this friendship to experience life and growth?

- Which is the most challenging for you: friendship with God, friendship with self, or friendship with others? Why do you think that is? Which could use a little more investment?

- As you look at your leadership context, which role set defines the majority of your leading relationships: peer leading peer, leading someone higher in the hierarchy, or leading someone lower in the hierarchical structure? How have you experienced the possibilities of Friendship Leadership within these roles? How would you like to further build up friendship within these role sets of leadership?

## Part III: Empowering Friendship Leadership

### Chapter 7: When Friendship Hurts

- Think of a time when you were hurt by friendship. How did you respond? How have you grown through that experience? How have you healed?

- As a leader, what is your greatest fear when it comes to bringing friendship into the relationship?

- Think of someone who leads you, what is one fear holding you back from deepening the relationship? What would God say to you about that fear?

### Chapter 8: Dual Relationships

- Describe a time when a lack of boundaries created issues in your sphere of leadership.

- Is the prohibition of all dual relationships realistic or unrealistic in your context? Why?

- How can you have "healthy" dual relationships?

## Chapter 9: Friendship Leadership in High Power Distance Cultures

- Would you describe your context (either within corporate or societal culture) as high or low power distance? Is your organization more vertical with stratified levels of positions or horizontal with every person being on somewhat equal footing in positional power? How does this affect the creation of friendships?

- Have you ever felt you were unable to form relationships in your context because of cultural barriers? Take some time now to pray to discover ways to offer love and respect, vulnerability and intimacy, even while you lead.

- Write out a list of ten creative ways to invest in Friendship Leadership in your context, while paying special attention to the opportunities and limitations of the culture in which you serve.

## Chapter 10: Cross-Attraction Friendship Leadership

- Take some time to reflect on those in your sphere of influence. Are there individuals being left out of the possibility of Friendship Leadership? Are there ways to build up these friendships in a healthy way?

- Perhaps you are the one feeling like friendship is a privilege being denied you. How can you take creative steps to address this in your own life? Is there a place where you could take more initiative?

- Take some time to have an honest conversation with a spouse or accountability partner. In that time, discuss the following points:

  - What fears do you have when it comes to cross-attraction Friendship Leadership?

  - Where might it be possible?

  - What are the non-negotiable boundaries? Is there a way to respect those without harming the people you're supposed to be building up as a leader?

  - Where have you allowed fear to prevent you from building up the family of God?

• Together, pray about and discuss some creative options for the healthy investment in cross-attraction Friendship Leadership.

## Chapter 11: The Introverted Leader Friend

- If you're an introvert yourself, consider the following questions:

  • Have you felt certain aspects of leadership were unavailable to you because of your personality? How has this chapter challenged that feeling? Do you see more possibilities now, given the strengths of your personality?

  • Have you ever used your personality as an excuse to avoid personal relationships with those you're leading? Instead of avoidance, what might be a better course of action?

  • What are your "restorative niches"? How can you plan them into your day so as you have more relational energy for Friendship Leadership?

  • What are some next steps you can plan to creatively pursue Friendship Leadership through the strengths found within your personality?

- If you're an extrovert, how do you engage with the introverts within your sphere of leadership? How has this chapter encouraged you to see a different side of the social dynamic of Friendship Leadership?

## Chapter 12: Conclusion

- How will you incorporate Friendship Leadership in your sphere of influence?
- What barriers will you face within your organization?
- What barriers must you overcome within yourself?
- What is one thing you will do now to get started?

# Bibliography

Aristotle. *Nicomachean Ethics.* Translated by Martin Ostwald. Upper Saddle River, NJ: Prentice Hall, 1962.

Benner, D. G. *Sacred Companions: The Gift of Spiritual Friendship and Direction.* Downers Grove, IL: InterVarsity, 2002.

Black, Hugh. *The Art of Being a Good Friend: How to Bring Out the Best in Your Friends and in Yourself.* Manchester, NH: Sophia Institute, 1999.

Cain, Susan. *Quiet: The Power of Introverts in a World that Can't Stop Talking.* New York: Broadway Paperbacks, 2013.

Carnegie, Dale. *How to Win Friends and Influence People: Revised Edition.* New York: Pocket Books, 1981.

Carter, Matt, and Aaron Ivey. *Steal Away Home: Charles Spurgeon and Thomas Johnson, Unlikely Friends on the Passage to Freedom.* Nashville: B&H Publishing Group, 2017.

Christianity Today. "C.S. Lewis: A Gallery of Family and Friends." Accessed December 4, 2017. http://www.christianitytoday.com/history/issues/issue-7/cs-lewis-gallery-of-family-

Conway, J. *Friendship.* Grand Rapids: Zondervan, 1989.

Cook, Jerry, and Stanley C. Baldwin. *Love, Acceptance, and Forgiveness: Being Christian in a Non-Christian World.* Grand Rapids: Bethany House, 1979.

Corey, Benjamin L. "Christian Ghosting: The Destructive Christian Practice We Don't Talk About." *Progressive Christian* (blog), *Patheos.com*, July 19, 2017, http://www.patheos.com/blogs/formerlyfundie/christian-ghosting-destructive-christian-practice-dont-talk/.

"Country Comparison." *Hofstede Insights.* Accessed December 18, 2017. https://www.hofstede-insights.com/country-comparison/.

Crossin, John W. *Friendship: The Key to Spiritual Growth.* Mahwah, NJ: Paulist, 1997.

"C.S. Lewis: A Gallery of Family and Friends." *Christian History* 7 (1985). https://christianhistoryinstitute.org/magazine/article/lewis-gallery-of-family-and-friends.

Emerson, Ralph Waldo and Lewis Mumford. *Friendship: Essays and Journals.* Garden City, NY: Doubleday, 1968.

Engstrom, Ted W. and Robert C. Larson. *The Fine Art of Friendship: Building and Maintaining Quality Relationships.* Nashville: T. Nelson, 1985.

Fehr, Beverley Anne. *Friendship Processes.* Thousand Oaks, CA: Sage, 1996.

Fernando, Ajith. *Reclaiming Friendship.* Leicester, England: Inter-Varsity, 1991.

Ford, Gary George. *Ethical Reasoning in the Mental Health Professions.* Boca Raton, FL: CRC Press, 2001.

Ford, Linda. "William Penn's Views on Women: Subjects of Friendship." *Quaker History* 72 (Fall 1983) 75–102.

Hill, Wesley. "C.S. Lewis' Deep Friendship With Arthur Greeves." *Preaching Today.* Accessed August 30, 2018. https://www.preachingtoday.com/illustrations/2016/october/5102416.html.

Hofstede, Geert, Gert Jan Hofstede, and Michael Minkoc. *Cultures and Organizations: Software for the Mind.* 3rd ed. New York: McGraw-Hill, 2010.

House, Robert J., et al., eds. *Culture, Leadership and Organizations.* Thousand Oaks, CA: Sage, 2004.

Houston, James M. "Prayer and Spiritual Friendship." *Knowing & Doing* (2001) 1-2. http://www.cslewisinstitute.org/webfm_send/653.

———. *The Transforming Friendship.* Oxford: Lion, 1989.

Isaacs, Florence. *Toxic Friends, True Friends: How Your Friends Can Make or Break Your Health, Happiness, Family, and Career.* New York: W. Morrow, 1999.

Jean, "what I'm Reading: CS Lewis' letters to Arthur Greeves," *in all honesty* (blog), October 14, 2013, http://jeaninallhonesty.blogspot.com/2013/10/what-im-reading-cs-lewis-letters-to.html.

Keaton, M. M. "Friendship as Communion with God." *Catechist* 3 (February 2002) 35.

Kunze, Bonnelyn Young. "Religious Authority and Social Status in Seventeenth-Century England: The Friendship of Margaret Fell, George Fox, and William Penn." *Church History* 57 (June 1988) 170-86.

Kushner, Harold S. *Living a Life That Matters: Resolving the Conflict Between Conscience and Success.* New York: Alfred A. Knopf, 2001.

Lewis, C. S. *The Four Loves.* Orlando: Harcourt Brace, 1988.

Lewis, C. S. *They Stand Together: The Letters of C.S. Lewis to Arthur Greeves (1914-1963).* Edited by Walter Hooper. London: Macmillan, 1979.

Lingenfelter, Sherwood G., *Leading Cross-Culturally: Covenant Relationships for Effective Christian Leadership.* Grand Rapids: Baker Academic, 2008.

———. *Transforming Culture: A Challenge for Christian Missions.* Grand Rapids: Baker Academic, 1998.

McClain, Boston, interviewed by Rachel McMurray-Branscombe, December 9, 2017.

McGinnis, Alan Loy. *The Friendship Factor: How to Get Closer to the People You Care For.* Minneapolis: Augsburg, 2004.

Meilaender, Gilbert. *Friendship: A Study in Theological Ethics.* Notre Dame, IN: University of Notre Dame, 1981.

Messner, Matthew. "Leadership That Cares: How Intentional Friendship Revolutionizes Leadership." PhD diss., Gordon-Conwell Theological Seminary, 2005.

Mills, Kathi. "Who Ministers to the Minister?" *Pastor's Family Magazine,* January 1996.

"Our Life," *Sisters of St. Benedict St. Mary Monastery* (blog), *Smmsisters.org,* accessed December 4, 2017, http://www.smmsisters.org/who-we-are/our-life.

Pakaluk, Michael, ed. *Other Selves: Philosophers on Friendship.* Indianapolis: Hackett, 1991.

Plueddemann, Jim. *Leading Across Cultures: Effective Ministry and Mission in the Global Church.* Downers Grove, IL: IVP Academic, 2009.

Rawlins, William K. *Friendship Matters: Communication, Dialectics, and the Life Course.* New Brunswick, NJ: AldineTransaction, 1992.

Rubin, Lillian B. *Just Friends: The Role of Friendship in Our Lives.* New York: Harper & Row, 1985.

Sanders, Randolph K., ed. *Christian Counseling Ethics: A Handbook for Therapists, Pastors & Counselors.* Downers Grove, IL: InterVarsity, 1997.

Sanders, Tim. *Love Is the Killer App: How to Win Business and Influence Friends.* New York: Random House, 2003.

Stade, G., ed. *Essays and Poems by Ralph Waldo Emerson.* New York: Barnes & Noble, 2004.

Stanley, Andy. *Deep and Wide: Creating Churches Unchurched People Love to Attend.* Grand Rapids: Zondervan, 2012.

The Order of St. Benedict, "CHAPTER THIRTY-THREE: OF A MIRCALE WROUGHT BY HIS SISTER SCHOLASTICA." *Book Two of the Dialogues: Life of Saint Benedict* (blog), *Osb.org*, February 14, 2005, http://www.osb.org/gen/greg/dia-35. html#P190_81319.

Thrall, Bill, Bruce McNicol, and Ken McElrath, eds. *The Ascent of a Leader.* San Francisco: Jossey-Bass Publishers, 1999.

Tracy, Diane, and Willian J. Morin. *Truth, Trust, and the Bottom Line: 7 Steps to Trust-Based Management.* Chicago: Dearborn Financial, 2001.

Tremper, Karen Ann. "Credentialed Women in the Foursquare Church: An Exploration of Opportunities and Hinderances in Leadership." PhD diss., Fuller Theological Seminary, 2013.

Weatherhead, Leslie D. *The Transforming Friendship.* London: Epworth, 1942.

Wuthnow, R. *Sharing the Journey: Support Groups and America's New Quest for Community.* New York: Free Press, 1994.

Yager, Jan. *Who's That Sitting At My Desk?* Stamford, CT: Hannacroix Creek Books, 2004.